HORRIBLE HISTORIES

GROOVY GREEKS

TERRY DEARY
ILLUSTRATED BY **MARTIN BROWN**

■SCHOLASTIC

For Jean Longstaff, with thanks

Scholastic Children's Books,
Euston House, 24 Eversholt Street,
London, NW1 1DB, UK

A division of Scholastic Ltd
London ~ New York ~ Toronto ~ Sydney ~ Auckland
Mexico City ~ New Delhi ~ Hong Kong

First published in the UK by Scholastic Ltd, 1996
This edition published 2007

Some of the material in this book has previously been published in
Horrible Histories The Awesome Ancient Quiz Book

Text copyright © Terry Deary, 1996, 2001
Illustrations © Martin Brown, 1996, 2001
All rights reserved

10 digit ISBN 0 439 94402 3
13 digit ISBN 978 0439 94402 1

Printed in the UK by CPI Bookmarque, Croydon

10

The right of Terry Deary and Martin Brown to be identified as the author and illustrators of this work respectively has
been asserted by them in accordance with the Copyright, Designs and Patents Act, 1988.

This book is sold subject to the condition that it shall not, by way of trade or otherwise be lent, resold, hired out, or otherwise circulated
without the publisher's prior consent in any form of binding or cover other than that in which it is published and without a similar
condition, including this condition, being imposed on a subsequent purchaser.

Contents

Introduction 5
Groovy Greek timeline 7
The gruesome gods 10
Fight like a Greek 16
Petrifying plays and electrifying epics 24
The savage Spartans 38
The odd Athenians 46
The power of the Persians 53
Alexander the Great-er 61
Think like a Greek 64
Live like a Greek 77
Die like a Greek 90
Odd Olympics 101
Funny food 109
Groovy Greek growing-up 114
The Romans are coming 124
Epilogue 128
Grisly Quiz 129
Interesting Index 137

Introduction

History can be horrible. And do you know who to blame?

> ER... MR POPPLECRUMP, MY HISTORY TEACHER?

No, it's the Greeks!

> BUT THE ANCIENT GREEKS ARE DEAD AREN'T THEY?

> DUNNO. WAS IT IN THE NEWSPAPERS?

> NAH, IT WAS YEARS AGO

> WHAT? BEFORE MR POPPLECRUMP WAS BORN?

> WELL MAYBE NOT *THAT* LONG AGO

The Greeks invented history about 2,500 years ago...

> YEAH... BUT OUR TEACHER STILL MAKES US SUFFER IT
>
> BORING

Inventing history is just one of the things we have to thank them for. They had the idea for plays, for the Olympic Games – even the camera...

> THEY DON'T SOUND AS BORING AS TEACHER MAKES THEM
>
> THEY SOUND GROOVY!
>
> YEAH. THE GROOVY GREEKS
>
> SOUNDS LIKE A GOOD TITLE FOR A BOOK

Funny you should mention that. Here is a book on the groovy Greeks. A book that will tell you all the things that teacher doesn't tell you. The things you really want to know. The hilarious stories and the horror stories.

> 'SPECIALLY THE HORROR STORIES. KNOW ANY GOOD ONES?

Groovy Greek timeline

BC
1600 – 1200 First Greek civilizations, ruled by the mighty Mycenaean lords of Crete.
About 1180 The siege of Troy – Troy loses to the famous wooden horse trick.
About 1100 The state of Sparta starts.
776 First recorded Olympic games.
About 750 – 550 Greeks take to the seas and become great traders.
About 730 Greeks produce the first works of written poetry in the world. Groovy Homer is the most famous.
640 World's first roof tiles manufactured at Temple of Hera at Olympia.
About 600 Thales, the Greek scientist, announces that the entire earth is actually floating in water.
585 Scientist Thales predicts an eclipse of the sun.
About 550 First plays performed. King Croesus of Lydia has gold and silver coins made; the first coins with writing on them.

7

About 530 Peisistratus of Athens creates a library.

About 520 Alcmaeon of Croton finds out about the human body by cutting up dead ones – groovy, eh?

490 Persians invade Greece – beaten by Greeks at The Battle of Marathon.

486 The first comedy drama at Athens.

480 Xerxes of Persia attacks the Greeks. The battle of Thermopylae. Spartan heroes die.

460 Athens v Sparta and Persia.

431 – 404 Athens tries to get too bossy so the others fight the Peloponnesian War. Sparta becomes top dog.

430 Great Plague of Athens kills Athenian leader, Pericles, not to mention a quarter of all the Athenian people.

413 A defeat at Syracuse for the army of Athens followed by . . .

404 The Fall of Athens.

About 400 Greek army engineers invent the stomach bow – the first type of crossbow.

371 Spartans lose to new top dog, the Thebans.

336 Alexander the Great becomes king of Macedon when his dad is assassinated. In just ten years he conquers the old enemy, Persia.

330 Aristotle invents the 'camera obscura' — a sort of pinhole camera and the idea behind today's film and television — now that really was groovy!

323 Alexander the Great dies. His generals divide up his empire.

322 The end of democracy in Athens when the Macedons take over.

215 Archimedes invents war machines like the catapult — they keep the Romans out for three years.

213 Archimedes has mirrors set along the harbour walls — they dazzle the Romans and set fire to their boats... Romans delayed for a while but...

212 Here come the Romans.

146 Greece part of the Roman Empire.

AD
393 Romans abandon Olympic Games — they don't happen again for 1500 years.

The gruesome gods

Before the groovy Greeks came the mighty Mycenaean people, who ruled Greece. Their greatest palace was on the island of Crete – it was so posh the queen had the world's first flushing toilet. Then the palaces were wrecked and the Mycenaean way of life went too. No more flushing toilets. What went wrong? Was it. . .
- war and attack from outside
- earthquakes
- disease and plague
- drought and famine
- change of climate?

They've all been suggested by historians. But, like the disappearance of the dinosaurs, no one really knows for sure.

The *Dorian* people moved down into Greece. They forgot how to write so we don't know a lot about those days. Historians call them the *Dark* Ages.

So, without writing, the history was preserved in stories. And, as the years passed, the stories became wilder and more unlikely. Legends, in fact.

The Greeks loved horror stories best of all. One Greek writer said that Greek children should not be told stories like this one (just as grown-ups today say you should not watch certain horror films).

But this book is a Horrible History and this story has a PG rating.

Do *not* read this story if you suffer from nightmares – or at least read it with your eyes closed so you don't suffer the most gory bits.

YOU HAVE BEEN WARNED!

Bringing up baby

Cronos was the chief god. You'd think that would make him happy, but no. Somebody told him that one of his children would take his place.

'Can't have that,' Cronos complained. 'Here, Mrs Cronos, pass me that baby!'

'What for?'

'Never mind daft questions. Just pass me that baby.'

Mrs Cronos passed across their new-born child. 'Here! What you doin' of with that baby?' she cried.

'Eatin' it.'

'Eatin' it! You great greedy lummock. You've just had your tea. You can't be hungry again already.'

'I'm not hungry,' the great god growled. 'Just there's this prophecy about one of my children taking my throne. No kid, no take-over, that's the way I look at it.'

'You don't want to go takin' no notice of them horryscopes,' Mrs Cronos sighed.

'Don't pay to take chances is what I always say,' Cronos said smugly. 'Pass them indigestion tablets.'

Time passed, as time does, and Mrs Cronos had more baby gods. . . and Cronos ate every last one. Well, not the *very* last one. Mrs Cronos was getting fed up with his gruesome guzzling. 'I'll put a stop to his little game,' she smirked as she hid the new baby, Zeus, under her bed. She picked up a big rock, wrapped it in a baby blanket and dropped it in the cot.

In walked Cronos. 'Where is it?'

'In the cot.'

'Ugly little beggar, isn't he?' the head god said, squinting at the boulder.

'Takes after his father then,' Mrs Cronos mumbled.

'Crunchy as well,' her husband said, swallowing teeth.

'Probably cos he's *bolder* than the rest,' Mrs Cronos agreed.

Cronos sat down heavily on a royal couch. 'Ooooh! I think I've eaten someone who disagrees with me.'

'It's possible,' Mrs Cronos sniffed. 'A lot of people disagree with you, sweetheart.'

'Ooooh!' The god groaned and clutched his stomach. 'I think I'm going to be sick!'

'Not on the new carpet, my love. There's a bowl over there,' Mrs Cronos warned him.

Cronos gave a heavenly heave and threw up not just his stony snack, but all the other baby gods as well. 'Just goes to show,' Mrs Cronos smiled happily. 'You can't keep a good god down!'

And did the young gods grow up to overthrow their dreadful dad? What do you think?

Don't feel too sorry for Cronos. He'd killed his own father, Uranus, and scattered the bits into the oceans. Cronos and the old gods were driven out by Zeus and the new gods. These new gods were much more fun. They were really one big, unhappy family. Always arguing, fighting and doing nasty things to each other.

Zeus ruled the earth and the sky from his home on the top of mount Olympus. Of all the groovy gods, Zeus was the grooviest. In a competition he got the top job. When he wasn't flirting with human women he was frying somebody with a thunderbolt.

Zeus's brother, Poseidon, ruled the sea. A job for a real drip. Old Pos wasn't too happy with this because he was a bad loser. That's why he sulked and went stomping around, whipping up the seas with a fork and creating storms. What a stirrer!

A third brother, Hades, was the real loser. He won the job of ruling the underworld. That must have been hell!

Quick quiz
Prometheus, a young god, liked humans so he stole fire from the gods and gave it to men on earth. But top god, Zeus, punished men by creating something new and terrible on earth. What were these terrible things?
1 women
2 flies
3 teachers

Answer:
1 **Women!** The Greeks thought they were sly and lying. They attracted men so that men couldn't live without them — at the same time they were such a nuisance men couldn't live with them either. Women were a great help when it came to sharing a man's wealth but no help at all when he was poor. Of course this legend is utter nonsense — if you don't believe me then ask any woman.

Fight like a Greek

The wooden heads of Troy
Everybody knows the story of the wooden horse of Troy. But can you believe it? Those Trojan twits saw a wooden horse standing outside the gates of the city ...

I'VE GOT A GREAT IDEA. WHY DON'T WE BRING IT *INSIDE* THE CITY. WE CAN HAVE IT AS A SORT OF STATUE IN THE CENTRE OF THE CITY
NOT A LOT OF WOODEN STATUES ABOUT
WE'LL BE THE FIRST. START A NEW FASHION
OH, ALL RIGHT. LOOK, IT EVEN HAS WHEELS ON TO MAKE IT EASY
ALMOST AS IF THE GREEKS *WANTED* US TO TAKE IT INTO THE CITY
THOUGHTFUL OF THEM. VERY THOUGHTFUL
ER... PARIS. YOU DON'T THINK THIS COULD BE SOME SORT OF... WELL... TRICK, DO YOU? MUMMY DID SAY, 'BEWARE THE GREEKS BEARING GIFTS'
NAH! YOUR MOTHER NEVER TRUSTED NOBODY. 'ERE, GRAB THAT ROPE AND GIVE US A HAND

Everyone thinks it's a wonderful story. No one stops to ask, 'Would the Trojans really be that stupid?' But, if they *did* ask that question, the answer would have to be 'Yes.' If brains were gunpowder the Trojans wouldn't have had enough to blow their helmets off. Because they were tricked into letting the groovy Greeks into their city a *second* time.

That's right. Everyone knows about the wooden horse trick. Teachers forget to tell you about the *second* one over 800 years later in 360 BC. . .

Tricking a Trojan. . . again
Charidemus was fed up. He paced up and down in his tent and rubbed a strong hand through his greying hair. He complained, 'I'll never capture Troy. The walls are just too strong. . . and the Trojans don't look as if they're starving to death, do they?'

'No, sir,' his young lieutenant mumbled. 'Perhaps if we made a wooden horse and. . .'

Charidemus glared at him. 'Thank you. You are the fiftieth person to suggest that. The Trojans won't fall for that old trick again. Next time they'll just set fire to the wooden horse. Would you like to volunteer to sit inside it, eh? See if I'm right?'

The young man turned red and said, 'No, sir.'

He was relieved to hear someone approaching the tent. He jumped to the door.

'Password?'

'Ajax,' the man called.

The lieutenant opened the flap and said, 'Enter, friend.'

The guard stepped through, pulled on a short chain

and dragged a ragged man through after him. The guard stood to attention. 'Spy, sir. Caught him stealing food. Permission to execute him, sir?' he barked.

General Charidemus peered at the prisoner. The man's clothes were dusty but quite rich. 'Not yet, Captain. Leave us together.'

The guard saluted and strode out. Charidemus nodded to a cushion. 'Sit down,' he ordered. 'Your name?'

The prisoner grinned. 'Damon.' He was a wiry man with dark eyes that seemed to dart around and couldn't meet anyone else's gaze.

'And you've come out from Troy to steal our food? Are things that bad inside the city then?'

Damon smiled slyly. 'You Greeks eat better than the Trojans. Even before the siege the king gave us poor rations.'

'You don't like the king? Then why work for him?' the Greek general asked.

The prisoner shrugged. 'It's a job.'

Charidemus leaned forward. 'And if I offered you a job? A better paid and better fed job?'

Damon looked at his thumb and slowly placed it in his mouth. 'I'd be happy to work for you. I'd be loyal to you.'

The general's eyes were hard as iron as he replied, 'Oh, you'd be loyal, Damon. Men who betray me die... but they die very slowly.'

The prisoner squirmed on his cushion and gave a nervous smile. 'What do you want me to do?'

'I want you to be my wooden horse, Damon. Listen carefully and I'll tell you exactly what I want you to do . . .'.

It took a week for Charidemus to prepare the plan. His young lieutenant was nervous. As he tightened the buckle on his general's armour he asked, 'How do you know Damon won't betray us?'

The general tested the weight of his short sword. 'Damon is greedy but he's not stupid. He knows that we will take Troy sooner or later. If we have to wait too long to get inside he knows we'll be angry. We'll certainly kill the Trojan men – including him. But if he helps us he lives – and doesn't have to go to bed hungry any more.'

Charidemus slid the sword into his belt. 'Pass me my cloak.'

The young man took the large, filthy cloak and slid it over his general's wide shoulders. A hood covered the man's square head. He arranged the cloak to cover the weapons, dusted his hands and gave a nod. 'You'll pass as a poor traveller, sir.' The lieutenant changed too.

The general strode out of his tent and met a dozen men dressed the same way. No one spoke. Charidemus led the way from the torch-lit camp on to the stony road to Troy. A small man sat quietly on a horse and watched them approach.

'Is everything ready, Damon?' the general asked softly.

'It is,' the small man smiled. He turned his horse and walked slowly back towards the city gates. The Greek soldiers dragged their sandals and began to limp towards the enemy city.

'Who goes there?' a guard cried from a gate tower.

'Damon!' the traitor cried.

'Ah, so it is! What have you got with you?'

'The Greeks are growing careless. I went to their camp and found some of our captured men with just a single guard. I killed him and brought them back,' Damon lied. 'But let me in quickly. They're weak and sick!'

'Aye, Damon... oh, you'd better give the password.'

'Castor,' Damon said quickly.

The gates creaked slowly open. The man on the horse rode in – the soldiers trudged behind him.

21

As the gates closed the men stood in the shadow of the wall and shrugged off their cloaks. They climbed the stone stairways to the gate towers and the walls.

The Trojan defenders had no chance. They were looking for Greeks outside the walls – they didn't expect the attack to come from within.

Charidemus cut the throat of the last guard and let the limp body drop into the dark and dusty ditch that ran outside the wall. The Greeks gathered in the tower above the gate.

'Now we wait for the rest of our army. . .' the general began, but his lieutenant hurried to the walls and looked over. There was a rattle of stones on the road as a body of armed men arrived and halted.

'They're here, sir, but they're too early!' the young man gasped.

'Either that or they aren't *our* men,' Charidemus said.

'How can we tell in the darkness?'

'The password, man, the password . . . you know, "Wooden Horse". Quick! Challenge them,' the general ordered.

'Who goes there?' the lieutenant called.

'Friend!' came the reply.

'Give the password.'

After a moment a voice called, 'Castor!'

The Greeks looked at General Charidemus. 'Let them in. If we don't they'll raise the alarm before our men get here. Hide behind the gates. As soon as the last man is in, you come out. Kill them. Kill every last one!'

The Greeks trotted down the stairs to their positions while the general and his lieutenant turned the winches that opened the gates. There was the sound of marching feet, cries of surprise and fear, the clash of weapons, then the silence of death.

From the darkest shadow of the Trojan street a small man gave a grim smile as he sat astride his horse. A horse that had led the enemy into Troy . . . again.

Petrifying plays and electrifying epics

After the stories of gods there were stories of heroes – men who were almost as powerful as gods. The only difference was they were 'mortal' – they could die.

The stories about heroes were told as poems. They were sung in the palaces of ancient Greece. Then, after the dark ages, poems were written down. The oldest written poem was by the Greek, Homer. His poem, *The Iliad*, tells the story of the siege of Troy, a story of the heroes who fought to the death to get Helen back to her hubby, King Menelaus.

It was such a great story it is still told today.

The Greeks heard the poems read on stage while a group of dancers performed. Then a clever poet called Aeschylus came along and had a great idea. He put a second reader on stage. Now you had a 'play' – the first drama in the world. Another groovy Greek invention!

Another famous playwright was Euripides – say 'you-rippa-deeze' – whose name gave lot of joy to suffering students of Greek.

| KNOCK KNOCK | WHO'S THERE? | EURIPIDES | EURIPIDES WHO? | EURIPIDES TROUSERS SO YOU BETTER PAY FOR THEM | GAD |

Of course, like everything else in Greece, play-writing became a competition. You went to see which play was the best and would win the prize. But it wasn't like your local theatre where you can go and watch a pantomime at Christmas. Greek theatre...

- always had the same scenery
- was out in the open air
- had no actresses – only actors who also played the female parts
- had no action on stage – only people *talking about* the exciting bits – murders and all that happened off stage
- had the actors wearing face masks – and high platform shoes so they moved around very slowly.

OK... IN THE NEXT SCENE YOU HAVE TO PLAY SHORT PEOPLE

There were two types of play. Serious ones where lots of people died miserably – they were called 'tragedies'. Funny ones full of groovy jokes and rude bits – they were called 'comedies'.

Some of their favourite tragedies were about the Trojan War. Several writers told the same story. The skill was to tell it in an interesting way.

Playwright Aeschylus didn't write about the fighting at Troy – Homer's poem did that. Aeschylus looked at the story of the women left behind. Women like Clytemnestra – wife of the Greek leader, Agamemnon. If Clytemnestra had kept a diary of those exciting years, would it have looked like this . . . ?

Diary of a murder

Dear Diary,
   You'll never believe what my sister Helen has gone and done! She's run off with that nice young man, Paris. She's a sly one that Helen. Husband Menelaus away from the palace and she chats up young Paris. Disgusting, I call it. You'd never catch me flirting with a guest. Of course I've got three kids to worry about. I have to set them a good example. Anyway, they reckon she's off to a place called Troy. Still, it's better than Sparta. Nasty brutal place that Sparta. I always said she'd never stick it out.

TROY

   There'll be trouble, mark my words. My husband, Agamemnon, came storming in tonight. 'Have you heard what your Helen's gone and done now?' he snaps.
   'I've heard. Can't say I blame her. Nice young chap, that Paris.' I knew that would upset him. Turned redder than blood on a sacrificial altar. I won't have him saying anything against our Helen.

She's always been flighty — I don't mind saying it. But she is my sister and I won't have anyone else saying a word against her.

'Nice young chap!' he screeches. 'He was a guest. A GUEST!! He betrayed the trust of Menelaus. Nicked his wife while he was out hunting!'

'No need to shout,' I told him. 'You'll upset Iphigenia,' I said and patted our girl on the head.

'What's he on about, Mum?' Iphigenia asked.

'Your Auntie Helen's gone off to Troy with that nice Prince Paris,' I said.

'Oh, is that all?' she said and she went back to her sewing. Lovely girl our Iphigenia. Wish our other two, Orestes and Electra, were as good. Funny couple those two.

ORESTES AND ELECTRA

'Anyway,' Agamemnon says, 'There'll be trouble. Big trouble. They reckon we'll get a thousand ships and sail after her. Bring her back.'

'That'll take months!' I said.

'A Greek's got to do what a Greek's got to do,' he said. 'Now let me have a bit of supper, then I'll be off to organize the army.'

'Organize the army?' I said. 'Don't tell me you're going as well!'

'Going? Going? I'm leading the whole expedition. Menelaus is my brother, after all.'

That's Agamemnon all over. Getting into somebody else's fight. Just an excuse to go off and have a battle. Leaves me stuck here for months on end. It would serve him right if I did what Helen did and found myself a toy-boy. That would teach him. In fact I've had my eye on that Aegisthus for a while now...

AEGISTHUS

But no. Our Iphigenia would be upset. I'll just let Agamemnon get on with it. I hope he gets sea-sick

AUTUMN

I'll kill him! I will kill Agamemnon. You'll not believe what he's done. If I'd had a sword in my hand I'd have killed him there and then. But he's gone now. I'll just have to wait. If it takes six months or six years till he gets back, I'll have my revenge. I'll have his blood, I will.

I'll never forgive him. I know he had

problems. A thousand ships waiting to sail to Troy and they couldn't even get out of the harbour at Aulis. The wind kept blowing them back. Week after week.

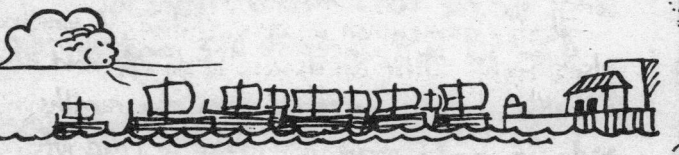

Of course, I knew that they went to the Oracle to ask for advice. But I never did find out what the Oracle told them. Very quiet he was when he came back.

'Well? What's to do?" I asked.

'Oh, a sacrifice,' he muttered. 'Just a sacrifice and the gods will turn the wind around'.

'That's all right then. What is it? A sheep? A Deer?'

He muttered something and started to leave the room. 'What was that?' I said. I'm not going deaf. I swear he didn't _want_ me to hear.

'Er... a maiden. We have to sacrifice a maiden,' he said, ashamed like.

'Eeh, our Agamemnon. You're never going to kill a little girl just to get that useless trollop Helen back, are you?'

'A Greek's got to do....'

'Yeah, what a Greek's got to do. I know. I think it's a wicked shame. I just feel sorry for the lass's mother, that's all.'

'Aye,' he said, sheepish like, and slipped out.

I was so upset. I have to say, I was upset at the thought of them brutes slaughtering a young girl just to keep some god happy. So I sent for our little Iphigenia to cheer me up.

Her nurse was pale as a marble statue when I called her. 'Iphigenia's gone for the sacrifice,' she said.

'Gone to the sacrifice!' I cried. 'She's too young to go watching horrible things like that. She'll be upset. It'll put her off her dinner. She's a fussy eater at the best of times,' I said.

'No,' the nurse mumbled. 'She won't be having any dinner any more. Iphigenia's gone for the sacrifice. She is the sacrifice,' the poor woman explained.

I was speachless. That double-crossing filthy rat of a husband had our little girl killed on an altar just so he could go off and play soldiers.

Of course the winds turned and he set sail before I could get my hands on him. Left me here with the 'funny couple', Orestes and Electra, to bring up.

But I can wait. Oh, I can wait. The waiting'll just make it all the nicer when I finally get him. But, believe me, I'll get him. If he doesn't get killed at Troy he'll get killed when he gets ~~home~~ back home. I can wait.

FIVE YEARS LATER

It's not as easy taking Troy as they expected. Their little game of soldiers isn't as exciting as they thought. Sitting outside the walls of Troy every day. They must be bored out of their tiny minds.

I was bored myself. But now I've got that nice, sensible Aegisthus to keep me company — sensible enough not to go to Troy.

It'll serve Agamemnon right if he gets killed. But now I've got Aegisthus to help me it's <u>certain</u> the old fool will be killed if he ever gets home. I've now got <u>two</u> reasons to get rid of him. I still haven't forgotten Iphigenia.

As for the 'funny couple', they're as strange as ever. Sometimes I think they don't love their Mother at all. That's fine, because I don't think much of them either.

ANOTHER FIVE YEARS LATER

So he's home. The conquering hero's home. Couldn't beat the Trojans in a fair fight so he beat them with a trick horse or something. Hid soldiers inside a wooden horse, they say.

WOODEN HORSE

Typical sneaky trick from Agamemnon. Poor Helen's back with Menelaus and everybody's happy... except me. And the Trojans of course

I pretended to welcome Agamemnon back like a loving wife, didn't I? But it was difficult when that girl stepped forward. 'This is Cassandra,' he said.

'Cassandra? Isn't she the King of Troy's daughter?'

'She is – and she is my wife-to-be,' he smirked.

'You've got a wife. You've got _me_!'

'Cassandra will be my second wife,' he said and marched into the palace. That scrawny girl trailed after him. They say she has the gift of prophecy. In that case she knows that we're going to kill her too. I could see it in her eyes. She knows. She knows.

NEXT DAY

It's done. He's dead. We waited till he climbed into his bath. I walked in with the sword. I could have struck him from behind. But I wanted him to know what was going to happen — just as Iphigenia must have known ten years ago. Aegisthus finished him off. It was messy.

Cassandra was in her room. Waiting. As if she expected me. Perhaps she did. She didn't cry out or try to run away. She just closed her eyes and bowed her head.

It was harder than killing him in a way. Still, it's over now. Oh, yes, Electra and Orestes, the funny people, have had their heads together, hatching some kind of plot. They can't do anything. It's against every law of god or man to kill your own mother. I'm safe.

> Dear Diary
>   It is against every law of god and man to kill your husband. And the gods would want us to avenge our father's death. We killed her and her murdering lover Aegisthus. Now we await the judgement of the gods for our crime.
>
>   Orestes and Electra.

The gods decided to destroy Orestes and Electra for killing their mother and sent the 'Furies' after them — sort of avenging angels. In the end the goddess, Athena, gave them a pardon.

That was the sort of story the Greeks liked to watch on the stage. People say that today's films and television programmes are too violent. But the truth is, entertainment has provided violent stories for thousands of years.

The truth about Troy
But was the story of Troy a 'history' story? Did it really happen? Homer was writing hundreds of years after the event. Of course, the story could have been passed down by word of mouth through the Dark Ages. Ask a historian . . .

Panel 1:
— WAS THERE A PLACE CALLED TROY?
— YES. ARCHAEOLOGISTS HAVE FOUND THE SITE OF THE RUINS

Panel 2:
— RUINS? SO WAS IT DESTROYED BY WAR?
— IT WAS DESTROYED AND REBUILT SEVERAL TIMES ONCE IT WAS DESTROYED BY AN EARTHQUAKE

Panel 3:
— DID HELEN OF TROY REALLY EXIST?
— DON'T KNOW. BUT IT WASN'T UNUSUAL FOR RAIDERS TO CARRY OFF QUEENS. SHE *COULD* HAVE EXISTED

Panel 4:
— AND WHAT ABOUT THE SACRIFICE OF IPHIGENIA?
— POSSIBLE. THERE WERE CERTAINLY CASES OF CHILDREN BEING SACRIFICED — AND EVEN PARTLY EATEN — IN THOSE DAYS

Panel 5:
— YEUCH! WHAT ABOUT THE WOODEN HORSE?
— INTERESTING, THAT ONE. IT COULD HAVE BEEN A POETIC IDEA FOR A WOODEN BATTERING-RAM

Panel 6:
... IT WOULD HAVE HAD A COVER TO KEEP THE DEFENDERS' ARROWS OFF THE ATTACKERS. THE COVER COULD HAVE BEEN HORSE-SHAPED

Don't tell tales

As well as plays, the ancient Greeks liked a good story. And nobody told better stories than Aesop. They are still popular today. Everybody's heard of *The Tortoise and the Hare*. The moral of that story is, 'Slow and steady wins the race'. Or *The Boy who Cried Wolf*, the moral of this story being, 'No one believes a liar – even if they start telling the truth.'

He gave us wise proverbs like, 'Never count your chickens before they're hatched'. But the most terrible tale of all is about Aesop himself.

Aesop was a Greek folk hero wno is supposed to have lived in the 6th century BC. One legend says he was born in Thrace, lived for a while as a slave on Sámos Island, was set free and travelled round the other states telling his stories.

Then he arrived at Delphi where the Oracle was. In ancient Greece, a priest or priestess who passed on advice from the gods was called an Oracle. Aesop seems to have upset the priests of the Oracle. Maybe he told the story of . . .

The man and the wooden god

In the old days, men used to worship sticks and stones and idols, and prayed to them to give them luck. It happened that a man had often prayed to a wooden idol he had received from his father, but his luck never seemed to change. He prayed and he prayed, but still he remained as unlucky as ever.

One day in the greatest rage he went to the wooden god, and with one blow swept it down from its stand. The idol broke in two, and what did he see? An immense number of coins flying all over the place.

And the moral of the story is, 'Religion is just a con trick created to make money for the priests.'

Whatever Aesop said, the priests didn't like it one little bit. They took him to the top of a cliff and threw him down to his death.

The savage Spartans

The first great state to grow after the Dark Ages was Sparta. The Spartan people were a bit odd. They believed they were better than anyone else. If the Spartans wanted more land then they just moved into someone else's patch. If someone was already living there the Spartans just made them slaves. In short, they were the ungrooviest lot in the whole of Greece.

> YOU HAVE A CHOICE, GIVE UP ALL YOUR LAND AND POSSESSIONS AND BECOME OUR SLAVE, OR WE KILL YOU

> HMM... TRICKY ONE

Of course, a lot of people didn't enjoy being slaves. They argued with the Spartans in the only language the Spartans knew – the language of violence. They were probably the toughest of the Greek peoples because they were always having to fight to prove how good they were.

But it wasn't enough to train young men to fight. The training started from the day you were born.

Ten foul facts
1 Children were trained for fitness with running, wrestling, throwing quoits and javelins – and that was just the girls!
2 Girls also had to strip for processions, dances and temple services. That way they wouldn't learn to show off with fine clothes.

3 The marriage custom of Sparta was for a young man to pretend to carry his bride off by violence. The bride then cut off her hair and dressed like a man. The bridegroom rejoined the army and had to sneak off to visit his new wife.

4 A new-born baby was taken to be examined by the oldest Spartans. If it looked fit and strong they said, 'Let it live.' If it looked a bit sickly it was taken up a mountain and left to die.

5 A child didn't belong to its parents – it belonged to the State of Sparta. At the age of seven a child was sent off to join a 'herd' of children. The toughest child was allowed to become leader and order the others about. The old men who watched over them often set the children fighting amongst each other to see who was the toughest.

6 At the age of 12 they were allowed a cloak but no tunic. They were only allowed a bath a few times a year.

THAT THASOS IS A CLEANLINESS FREAK

YEAH...THAT'S HIS THIRD BATH THIS YEAR

7 Children slept on rushes that they gathered from the river bank themselves. If they were cold in winter then they mixed a few thistles in with the reeds . . . the prickling gave them a feeling of warmth.

8 The Spartan children were kept hungry. They were then encouraged to steal food – sneakiness is a good skill if you're out on a battlefield. If they were caught stealing they'd be beaten. They weren't beaten for stealing, you understand – they were beaten for being careless enough to get caught. Sometimes the young men were beaten just to toughen them up. If the beating killed the youth then it was just bad luck.

> YOU SHOULD BE A LOT TOUGHER NOW... DEAD, BUT TOUGHER

9 Older boys had younger boys to serve them. If the younger boy did something wrong then a common punishment was a bite on the back of the hand.

10 If you cried out while you were fighting then not only were you punished but your best friend was punished as well.

Of course, the savage Spartans were no worse than some of their enemies, such as the Scythians. The historian, Herodotus (485 – 425 BC), described the horrors of the Scythians . . .

> *In a war, it is the custom of a Scythian soldier to drink the blood of the first man he kills. The heads of all enemies killed in battle are taken to the king; a head represents a token which allows the soldier a share in the loot – no head no loot. He strips the skin off the head by*

> *making a circular cut round the ears and shaking out the skull; then he scrapes the flesh off the skin with an ox's rib, and when it is clean works it supple with his fingers. He hangs these trophies on the bridle of his horse like handkerchiefs and is very proud of them. The finest warrior is the one who has the most scalps. Many Scythians sew scalps together to make cloaks and wear them like the cloak of a peasant.*

The boy who didn't cry 'fox'
One Spartan story shows you how peculiar the Spartans really were. It's a story about a good little Spartan boy.

How to be a good Spartan 1: Pinch whatever you like – but don't get caught
He stole a fox cub belonging to somebody else.

How to be a good Spartan 2: Don't give up without a struggle
The boy was seen running away from the scene of the theft and arrested. But before they caught him he just had time to stuff the fox cub up his tunic.

How to be a good Spartan 3: Cheat, lie and trick your way out of trouble
The boy's master asked the boy where the fox cub was. The boy replied, 'Fox cub? What fox cub? I don't know anything about a fox cub!'

How to be a good Spartan 4: It's better to be a dead hero than a live whinger
The master's questioning went on . . . and on. Until suddenly the boy fell down. Dead. When the guards examined the body they found the fox cub had eaten its way into the boy's guts. The tough Spartan lad hadn't given any sign that he was suffering and he hadn't given in, even though it cost him his life.

Could you be as boldly deceitful as the Spartan boy?

LOOKS LIKE HE CHOKED ON HIS UNFINISHED MATHS HOMEWORK

Thermopylae
The story of the boy and the fox might not be true – it simply shows the sort of people the Spartans admired. But the story of the battle of Thermopylae is almost certainly true. Again it shows the Spartans dying rather than giving in.

There were just 300 Spartans led by King Leonidas defending the narrow pass of Thermopylae against tens of thousands of Persians. The Persian leader, Xerxes, sent spies to report how many soldiers were defending the pass. He couldn't believe the Spartans would be daft enough to fight and die. Xerxes didn't know the Spartans.

But the Spartans were not just unafraid. They were really cool about it. They spent the time before the battle oiling their bodies and combing their hair – now that *was* groovy.

> OH NO! I'VE GOT MY SPEAR-OIL MIXED UP WITH MY-TORSO WAX

How to be a good Spartan 5: When you're in trouble, think of something witty to say

The Spartans were warned that the Persians had so many archers that their arrows would blot out the sun. Dioneces, the Spartan general, said, 'That's good. We'll have a bit of shade to fight the battle.'

> HOW'S THINGS MELOS?

> OH, NOT BAD PAROS... CAN'T COMPLAIN

How to be a good Spartan 6: Stay cooler than an iced lolly

The Spartans held on for a week. Then a traitor guided the Persians to a secret pathway that led them behind the Spartans. The 300 Spartans were massacred. As they fought to the death some lost their swords. They battled on with their fists and their teeth.

Could you stay as cool as a Spartan in danger?

YOU'RE LATE!

WELL, THERE'S EIGHT OF US IN THE FAMILY AND THE ALARM WAS SET FOR SEVEN...

Did you know . . . ?
One horrible historical way of proving you were a good Spartan was to be whipped at the altar of the god, Artemis. The one who suffered the most lashes was the toughest. Bleeding half to death – sometimes *all the way* to death – but *tough*. Ah yes, a *perfect* Spartan.

The spooky Spartan

Pausanius was a great Spartan general who helped to defeat the Persians in 479 BC. But the Spartans thought he was getting too big-headed and they asked him to return to Sparta to explain – or be punished.

Pausanius was not amused. He wrote to the Persian king, Xerxes, and offered to betray Sparta. Off went the messenger to Xerxes. But that messenger wondered why other messengers before him hadn't come back. So he opened the letter and read it. There on the end was a little message for Xerxes . . .

> blah blah blah
> blah blah, blah
> blah...
>   lots of love
>   Pausanius
> P.S. Kill the messenger so he can't talk.

Oo.

The messenger took the letter to the Spartans instead of to Xerxes – wouldn't you? The Spartans sent a force to kill Pausanius. The general fled to the temple of Athena where he sheltered in a small building. 'You can't lay a finger on me here. I'm on sacred ground,' he said.

'Right,' the leader of the assassins said. 'We won't lay a finger on you.' And they didn't. They just bricked up the door and left him to starve to death. That should have been the end of Pausanius. The trouble was his ghost started wandering round the temple making such hideous noises that the priestess was losing customers. In the end she sent for a magician – a sort of groovy Greek Ghostbuster – to get rid of him . . . finally.

The odd Athenians

Deadly Draco
The people of Athens were very different from the Spartans. One of their first rulers was a man called Draco. The Athenians thought the Spartans were pretty brutal, but the laws of Draco were nearly as cruel. He wrote the first law book for Athens, and criminals were executed for almost any crime. Under Draco's laws...
- you could have someone made your personal slave if they owed you money
- the theft of an apple or a cabbage was punishable by death
- people found guilty of idleness would be executed.

Draco said...

> Yes, it's unfair. Little crimes and big crimes get the same punishment. If only I could think of a punishment worse than death for the serious ones.

Seven hundred years later a Greek writer, Plutarch, said . . .

> *Draco's laws were not written in ink but in blood.*

Other Greeks thought that Draco's laws were better than no laws. (The people who thought this were not the ones who Draco had executed, of course.)

Playful Peisistratus

Another ruler, Peisistratus, wasn't so quite so harsh. He was still a 'tyrant' – in Greece that was someone who took control of the state by force – but he stayed there only as long as the people agreed with what he was doing.

Peisistratus made the people pay heavy taxes – ten per cent of all they earned – but at least he had a sense of humour.

One day he visited a farmer. The farmer didn't recognize Peisistratus.

'WHAT DO YOU GET OUT OF THIS LAND?'

'NOTHING BUT ACHES AND PAINS, I WISH PEISISTRATUS WOULD TAKE HIS TEN PER CENT OF THOSE'

Peisistratus laughed – and ordered that the old farmer need never pay taxes again.

Plotting Peisistratus

Peisistratus became very unpopular and the people of Athens were turning against him. Then one day he drove his cart into the market place in a terrible state. He and his mules were cut and bleeding. 'I've been attacked by assassins!' he cried. 'I barely escaped with my life.'

HOW COME HE GETS ALL THE ATTENTION?

The Athenians were worried they would lose their leader – not a popular leader, but the only leader they had. They organized the strongest and most brutal Athenian men to be his bodyguards. He then used them to seize control of the city.

The attack on Peisistratus had put him in power. Just as he meant it to. For there had been *no* attack. The crafty leader had simply made the wounds himself!

Who killed the ox?

The Athenians weren't as ruthless as the Spartans. But they had their own funny little ways. One of the strangest customs of Athens involved the sacrifice of an ox in the temple. Killing the ox wasn't strange in itself. It's what the Athenians did *afterwards* that was curious. They held a trial to decide, 'Who killed the ox?'

I BLAME THE GIRLS WHO CARRIED THE WATER THAT SHARPENED THE AXE!

WE BLAME THE MAN WHO SHARPENED THE AXE AND THE KNIFE

I BLAME THE MAN WHO TOOK THE KNIFE AND THE AXE

I BLAME THE MAN WHO HIT THE OX WITH THE AXE

I BLAME THE MAN WHO STABBED THE OX WITH THE KNIFE

I BLAME THE KNIFE

WHAT HAVE YOU GOT TO SAY FOR YOURSELF, KNIFE?

IN THAT CASE I FIND THE KNIFE GUILTY OF THE OX'S MURDER. I SENTENCE THE KNIFE TO DEATH BY DROWNING. THROW THE KNIFE IN THE SEA

TO BE BLUNT I CAN'T SEA THE POINT

Horrible hemlock

The Athenians didn't just have strange ways of killing knives. They also killed each other in unusual ways.

After they had lost the war with Sparta the Athenians looked for someone to blame. They blamed the old teacher, Socrates. Being a rather groovy guy, he was always hanging around with young people, telling them not to believe in the old gods. (That's a bit like your own teacher telling you not to believe in Father Christmas.) In Athens this was punishable by death.

But the Athenians didn't kill the old teacher – they told him to kill himself with poison! Plato described the gruesome scene . . .

> *The man who was to give the poison came in with it ready mixed in a cup. Socrates saw him and said, 'Good Sir, you understand these things. What do I have to do?'*
>
> *'Just drink it and walk around until your legs begin to feel heavy, then lie down. It works very quickly.'*
>
> *The man gave Socrates the cup.*
>
> *The teacher took it cheerfully, without trembling, and without even turning pale. He just looked at the man and said, 'May I drink a toast?'*
>
> *'You may,' the man replied.*
>
> *'Then I drink to the gods and pray that we will be just as happy after death as we were in life.'*

Then he drank the poison quickly and cheerfully. Until then most of us had held back our tears. But when we saw him drinking, the tears came in floods. I covered my face and wept — not for him but for myself, I had lost such a good friend.

Socrates looked at us and said sternly, 'I have heard that a person should be allowed to die in silence. So control yourselves and be quiet.' We stopped crying.

The teacher lay down. The man with the poison squeezed his foot. Socrates said he felt nothing. He said that when the poison reached the heart he would be gone.

As the numbness reached his waist Socrates called to young Crito. He said, 'Crito, we owe Asclepius a sacrifice. Be sure you pay him. Don't forget.'

[Asclepius was the god of healing.]

'Of course,' Crito replied. 'Is there anything else you want?'

But Socrates didn't reply.

This was the end of our friend. The best, wisest and most honest person I have ever known.

What a hero! Probably the only teacher in history to die so nobly. Would your teacher be as brave?

Unfortunately you'll never have the chance to find out . . . Boots the Chemist does not sell hemlock.

Dreadful democracy

Most countries today are run as *democracies* — that is to say every adult has a vote on which laws are passed and how the government spends its money.

Athens, being really groovy, had the *first* democracy. But because they still had a lot to learn, they didn't quite get it right . . .

The power of the Persians

King Darius of Persia had a large army and decided it was about time he took over Greece as well. He didn't bother going to the battle personally – he thought the Greeks would be a pushover. They *should* have been a pushover because . . .

• there was only the Athenian army to stop them – the Spartans were too busy at a religious festival and they missed the battle

• the Greek soldiers were a bit frightened by the appearance of the Persian soldiers.

The Persians were wearing *trousers* while the Greeks wore groovy *skirts*.

Still, the Athenian Greeks won the great battle at a place called Marathon.

That kept the Persians away for about ten years.

Then along came the new Persian king, Xerxes, with an absolutely *huge* army.

There were too many soldiers to transport across the Hellespont – a stretch of water almost 1200 metres wide between Greece and Persia – so Xerxes built a bridge.

A storm came and smashed the bridge. Xerxes was cross – yes, I know there are *two* crosses in Xerxes, but I don't mean that sort of cross. He was furious.

So, what did the potty Persian do?

1 Ordered the bridge builder to be given three hundred lashes.

LASH! LASH!

2 Ordered the sea at Hellespont to receive three hundred lashes.

THRASH! THRASH!

3 Ordered the army to swim across.

SPLASH! SPLASH!

Answer: 2 Xerxes ordered that the sea should receive the lashes and have iron shackles thrown in as a punishment. One story even said he sent torturers to brand the sea with burning irons.

Paper-headed Persians

The Greeks wouldn't have feared the Persians so much if they'd known what the great historian Herodotus knew. He told a remarkable story about an earlier Persian battlefield – at Pelusium in Egypt where the Persians had fought in 525 BC.

> *On the battlefield I saw a strange thing which the natives pointed out to me. The bones of the dead lay scattered on the field in two lots — those of the Persians and those of the Egyptians. If, then, you strike a Persian skull (even with a pebble) they are so weak you will break a hole in them. But the Egyptian skulls are so strong that you may hit them with a rock and hardly crack them.*

The wooden wall

After slaughtering the Spartans, Xerxes headed south towards Athens. The Athenians retreated to the island of Salamis, just off the coast of Athens. They had to watch while Xerxes burned Athens to the ground.

But the Athenian leader was a groovy Greek called Themistocles. He went to the temple at Delphi and asked for advice from the 'Oracle' – a kind of adviser on behalf of the gods. The Oracle told him to 'put his trust in the wooden wall'. What did he do?

1 Build a navy (of wooden ships).
2 Build a wooden fence around the island of Salamis to keep the Persians out.
3 Build a wooden fence around Athens to keep the Persians in.

Answer: 1 Themistocles guessed that he should put his faith in his navy – and he got it right. The 800 Persian ships were attacked in the narrow waters between Salamis and Athens by just 310 Greek ships. The Greeks had bronze rams on their bows that smashed and sank the Persians.

The spooky ship of Salamis
Herodotus also reported a strange happening at the battle of Salamis . . .

> *The Athenians tell this story about a captain from Corinth called Adeimantus. As the battle started he was filled with fear and dread; he hoisted his sails and hurried from the fight. When the other Corinthians saw this they turned to follow him. But just as they reached the temple of Athena on Salamis, a ship came alongside them. It was a ship of the gods for no man sent it. A voice from the strange ship called, 'Would you betray your Greek friends, Adeimantus? They are now winning the battle. Turn back and help.' The Corinthian said it was a lie. The voice replied, 'You can take this ship and destroy it if you find out I am lying. Turn back, turn back.' So Adeimantus and the Corinthians joined the battle again and helped the Greeks to win. But no one was able to tell him where the strange ship had come from . . .*

Maybe it was a 'ghost ship'. Another story says the Corinthians only *pretended* to run away. It was all part of a cunning Athenian plan. The Corinthians' trick led the Persians into a trap. They then turned and attacked them when they least expected it. There never was a ship of the gods.

Which story do you believe? One fact is that lots of sailors died. Two horrible historical epitaphs read . . .

> HE WENT DOWN WITH HIS SHIP AND WHERE HIS BONES ARE ROTTING ONLY THE SEABIRD KNOWS

And . . .

> SAILORS, DON'T ASK WHOSE BODY LIES HERE. I WISH YOU BETTER LUCK THAN MINE AND A KINDER SEA

Peloponnesian wars

Xerxes the Persian went home after he lost the sea battle at Salamis. His son-in-law, Mardonius, wanted to stay and batter a few more Greeks, so Xerxes left him to get on with it. Mardonius was killed and his army defeated.

Of course, the Athenians were really pleased with themselves. They decided to get all the Greek states to team up in case the Persians ever came back. The trouble was the Athenians wanted to be the captain of the team.

Sparta weren't having that. They decided not to play. After that it was just a matter of time before Athens and Sparta fought each other to see who was best. And that was the start of the Peloponnesian War.

Awful armies
Alcibiades was a great Athenian general – but a terrible poser. He dressed in the grooviest clothes and would do anything to draw attention to himself. Once he cut off the tail of his favourite dog so that people would take notice.

> I WONDER IF THEY'D NOTICE HIM MORE IF I BIT HIS NOSE OFF?

Half of Athens (especially the women) loved him – but the men in power hated him and wanted him dead. They sent him off to fight the Spartans while they plotted against him.

Alcibiades led the Athenian army in the attack on the Spartan allies at Syracuse (in Sicily) between 415 and 413 BC. But he was called back to Athens because he was charged with 'sacrilege' – that's being nasty to the gods. He was supposed to have gone to some statues of gods and knocked off their noses – and (because the statues didn't have any clothes on) he knocked off their 'naughty bits' as well.

Of course, clever Alcibiades knew they'd probably kill him for this. So he *didn't* go back to Athens, sensible man. He went over to the enemy – *Sparta*. He told the Spartans all the secrets of the Athenian army. The Spartans went and helped Syracuse.

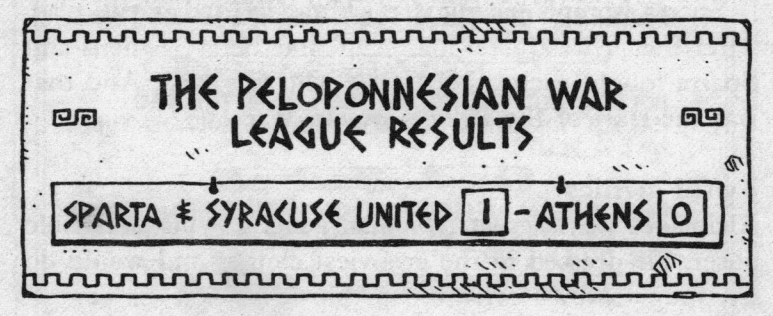

```
THE PELOPONNESIAN WAR
    LEAGUE RESULTS

SPARTA & SYRACUSE UNITED [ 1 ] - ATHENS [ 0 ]
```

Of course, Alcibiades came to a sticky end – just like the tail of his dog, really! The Spartans had him assassinated rather than let him switch back to fighting for Athens.

A group of men arrived at his house to kill him but hadn't the nerve to fight him face to face – even though they outnumbered him. First they set his house on fire. When Alcibiades came out into the open, carrying his sword, they shot him full of arrows from a safe distance.

Wonderful weapons
During the Peloponnesian wars, Greeks were fighting Greeks. If you know how your enemy fights, you can stop him – and at the same time he can stop you. Every battle becomes a 0–0 draw. What you need are some secret weapons to surprise and frighten the enemy.

That's what the groovy Greek army from Boetia came up with. Here's what they made . . .

TOP SECRET
THE BOETIAN BLASTER

1. CUT DOWN A TALL STRAIGHT TREE TRIM THE BRANCHES OFF THEN SPLIT THE TRUNK IN TWO

2. HOLLOW OUT THE TRUNK THEN JOIN THE TWO HALVES TOGETHER, YOU NOW HAVE A HOLLOW TUBE LIKE A FLUTE

3. HANG A METAL VESSEL FULL OF SMOULDERING COALS, TAR AND SULPHUR AT ONE END AND A BELLOWS AT THE OTHER END

4. CARRY THE MACHINE TO A PLACE WHERE THE ENEMY WALLS ARE MOSTLY MADE OF WOOD. AIM THE TUBE AT THE WALLS AND SQUEEZE THE BELLOWS.

   ← PROTECTION FROM ENEMY ARROWS

5. A HUGE FLAME WILL SHOOT OUT OF THE METAL VESSEL, SETTING FIRE TO THE WALLS AND DRIVING THE DEFENDERS AWAY

It worked! The Boetians captured the city of Delium with it. They had invented the world's first *flame thrower!*

Alexander the Great-er

Just when the Persian threat to Greece had begun to fade, a new one came from a small kingdom in the north of Greece called Macedon. Some historians have even said that Macedon wasn't Greek at all.

First came Philip, king of Macedon. He defeated the Athenians and then told them he wanted them to attack the old enemy . . . Persia.

Then there was a small hitch in Philip's plan . . . he died. But that was only a tiny complication for the plan. (A rather bigger complication for Philip, of course.) Philip's son was greater and even groovier than him. Alexander the Great-er in fact . . .

Alexander - This is Your Life

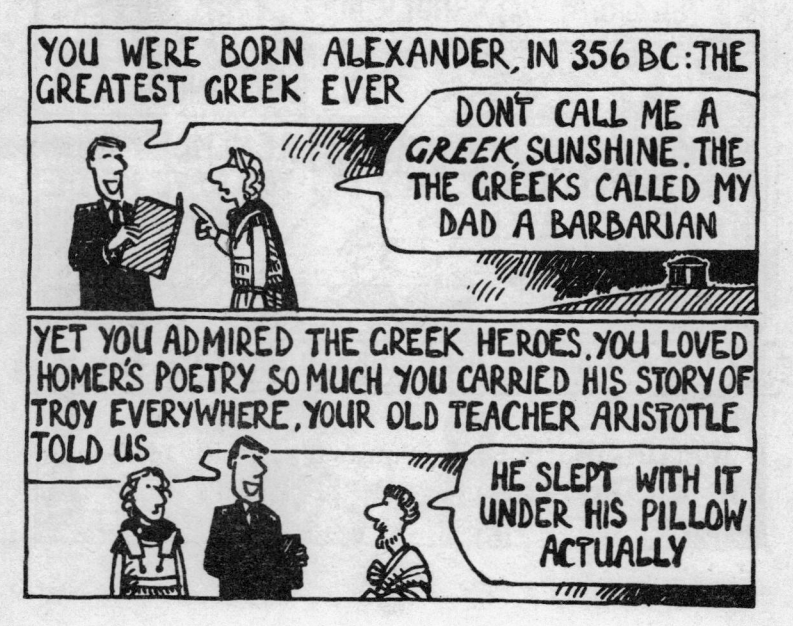

> YOU WERE BORN ALEXANDER, IN 356 BC: THE GREATEST GREEK EVER
>
> DON'T CALL ME A GREEK, SUNSHINE. THE THE GREEKS CALLED MY DAD A BARBARIAN

> YET YOU ADMIRED THE GREEK HEROES. YOU LOVED HOMER'S POETRY SO MUCH YOU CARRIED HIS STORY OF TROY EVERYWHERE. YOUR OLD TEACHER ARISTOTLE TOLD US
>
> HE SLEPT WITH IT UNDER HIS PILLOW ACTUALLY

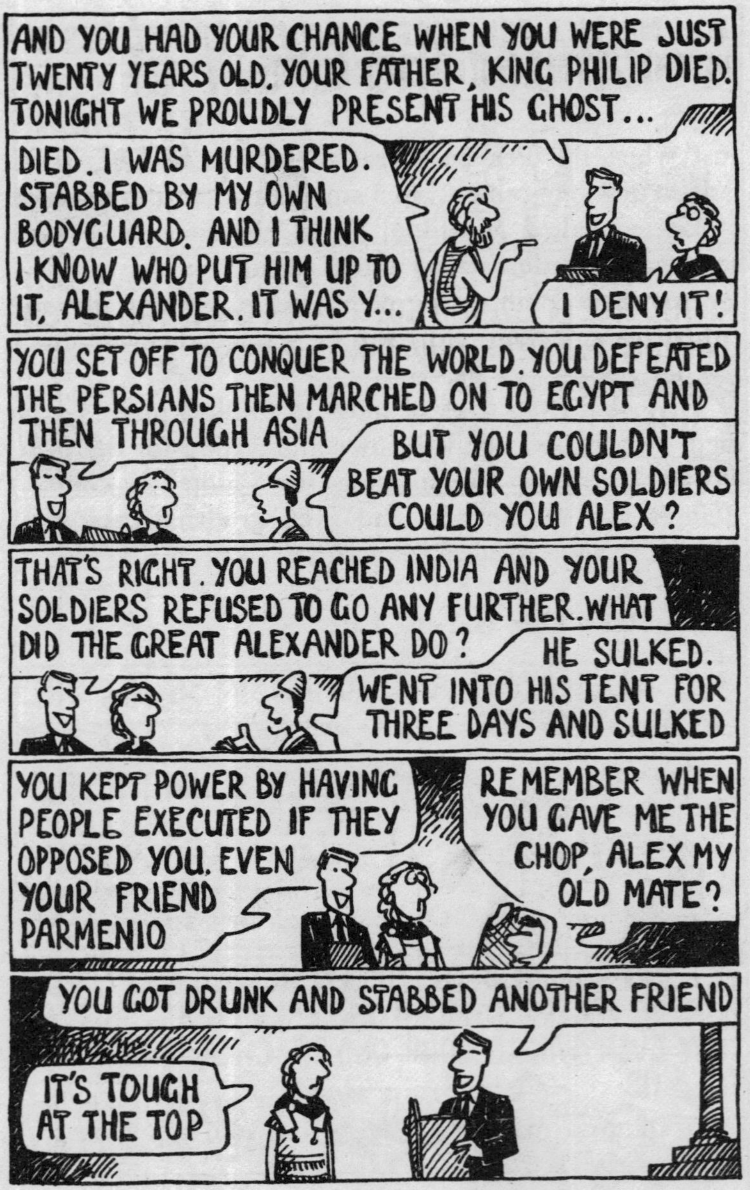
AND YOU HAD YOUR CHANCE WHEN YOU WERE JUST TWENTY YEARS OLD. YOUR FATHER, KING PHILIP DIED. TONIGHT WE PROUDLY PRESENT HIS GHOST...
DIED. I WAS MURDERED. STABBED BY MY OWN BODYGUARD. AND I THINK I KNOW WHO PUT HIM UP TO IT, ALEXANDER. IT WAS Y...
I DENY IT!
YOU SET OFF TO CONQUER THE WORLD. YOU DEFEATED THE PERSIANS THEN MARCHED ON TO EGYPT AND THEN THROUGH ASIA
BUT YOU COULDN'T BEAT YOUR OWN SOLDIERS COULD YOU ALEX?
THAT'S RIGHT. YOU REACHED INDIA AND YOUR SOLDIERS REFUSED TO GO ANY FURTHER. WHAT DID THE GREAT ALEXANDER DO?
HE SULKED. WENT INTO HIS TENT FOR THREE DAYS AND SULKED
YOU KEPT POWER BY HAVING PEOPLE EXECUTED IF THEY OPPOSED YOU. EVEN YOUR FRIEND PARMENIO
REMEMBER WHEN YOU GAVE ME THE CHOP, ALEX MY OLD MATE?
YOU GOT DRUNK AND STABBED ANOTHER FRIEND
IT'S TOUGH AT THE TOP

> YOU MARRIED THE MOST BEAUTIFUL PRINCESSES IN IN THE LANDS YOU CONQUERED...
>
> LIKE I SAY, IT'S TOUGH AT THE TOP

> ALEX—THAT WAS YOUR LIFE! SHAME, MY LOVE, BUT AT THE AGE OF 32, YOU GOT DRUNK ONCE TOO OFTEN, CAUGHT A FEVER AND DIED
>
> WHAT!

> YES, ALEXANDER THE GREAT, HERO, POETRY-LOVER, SOLDIER AND MURDERER... THAT WAS YOUR LIFE

The knotty problem

Alexander entered Gordium and was told that the wagon of King Gordius was tied to its shafts with a knot that no one could untie. A legend said that the man who finally untied it would rule all Asia. How did Alexander unfasten the wagon from its shafts?

Answer: He took out his sword and cut through the knot.

Think like a Greek

The Greeks were very superstitious people. They believed in horoscopes and ghosts and the gods deciding your fate. They believed that the gods spoke through 'Oracles' and you could learn about the future . . . if you understood the Oracle.

Awesome Oracles
The Greeks liked to know what would happen in the future. They didn't have crystal balls or people reading your palm. Instead they had Oracles. You went to a holy place, made a sacrifice and asked a god to tell you what the future held.

Of course, the god didn't speak to a human directly. There were a couple of ways of getting your message. At Delphi, the god Apollo spoke through his Oracle priestess. She was a bit like a medium in a seance today. She went into a trance and spoke in a strange language. The priests then took this baffling information and told the visitor what it meant.

> **WHAT DID SHE SAY?**
>
> **TEN DRACHMA AND A DEAD COW AND I'LL TELL YOU**
>
> **I'LL BE RIGHT BACK**
>
> **SO? WHO'LL WIN THE OLYMPIC FOOT RACE THIS YEAR?**
>
> **THE FIRST ONE TO CROSS THE FINISH LINE OF COURSE, TA-TA**

The priests at Delphi actually could give good advice. So many visitors came, with so much gossip, that the priests of Delphi knew more than most people about what was going on in the Greek states.

Croesus the crafty

There were several Oracles in Greece. Crafty King Croesus decided to test them to see which was the most accurate.

He sent seven messengers to seven Oracles. They all had to ask the same question at the same time... *What is King Croesus doing at this very moment?*

They brought their replies back to the king. The Oracle of Delphi's answer was a curious one. It said...

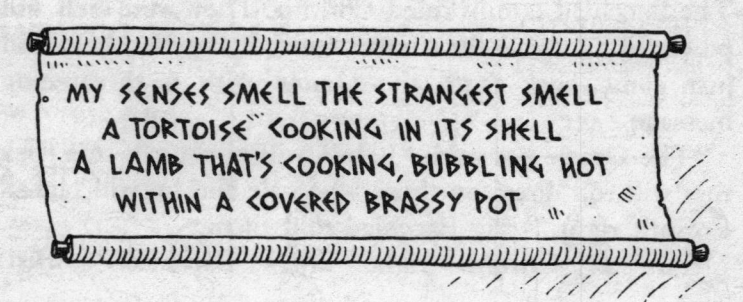

> MY SENSES SMELL THE STRANGEST SMELL
> A TORTOISE COOKING IN ITS SHELL
> A LAMB THAT'S COOKING, BUBBLING HOT
> WITHIN A COVERED BRASSY POT

Croesus was impressed. He'd deliberately chosen the daftest thing he could think of to do on that day. So he cut up a tortoise and a lamb and made a stew of them. He cooked them in a brass cauldron with a lid.

Croesus decided the Oracle of Delphi was the one to believe. Crafty Croesus. But. . .

Double-crossed Croesus

But the priests also cheated a bit. They gave curious answers that could mean more than one thing. King Croesus of Lydia spoke to the Oracle when he was about to go to war with Persia.

'What will happen if I attack Persia?' King Croesus asked.

'In the battle a great empire will be destroyed,' the Oracle said.

Croesus went off happily into battle – and lost! Lydia was destroyed. He thought the Oracle meant that *Persia* would be destroyed.

Some of the Greeks' favourite stories were about the Oracle. Many were about the ancient game of . . .

Beat the Oracle

The Bacchiad family ruled Corinth. They were rich and powerful . . . and they were worried. Big Bacchiad had just come back from the Oracle with a threatening message.

'The Oracle has said, "Labda will give birth to a rock that will roll down on those who rule and he will put all Corinth right,"' Big Bacchiad told them.

'Put all Corinth right?' Mrs Bacchiad sniffed.

'Nothing wrong with Corinth. . . at least, not while we're in charge.'

'That's not the point,' Little Bacchiad pointed out. 'If the gods say it's curtains for us, then it's curtains for us.'

'Hah! Just like a man, talking like that. Listen, if the Oracle says she's giving birth to the child who'll defeat us, we simply kill the child.'

'That's murder that is,' Big Bacchiad frowned. 'We'd never get away with it.'

'Not if the baby has an *accident*,' Mrs Bacchiad grinned an evil grin.

'Not much chance of that,' Little Bacchiad sighed.

'Oh, but there is if we *make* it have an accident,' the woman explained. 'As soon as the baby is born, we go visiting. Ask to see the new baby.'

'That's nice,' Big Bacchiad said.

'No it's not,' Mrs Bacchiad said with a slow shake of the head. 'Whoever she hands the baby to will drop it.'

'Drop it!' Little Bacchiad squeaked.

'On the stone floor,' the woman said grimly. 'On its head. End of problem.'

Of course it wasn't that simple. With the Oracle it never is. The baby was born and the Bacchiads went to visit. Mrs Bacchiad left the house ten minutes later. Her face was white with bright red spots of anger on her chubby cheeks.

'I cannot believe it. All you had to do was drop the baby. *Drop the baby!* That's what we agreed. Why did you not drop it?'

Big Bacchaid gave a faint and sheepish smile. 'It smiled at me. I couldn't drop the little feller while he was smiling at me, could I? I hadn't the heart.'

'Heart? It's not heart you're short of — it's brain,' the woman seethed. She turned to Little Bacchiad. 'Tonight you go back with a club. You creep into the house and you kill the child. Understand?'

Little Bacchiad nodded. 'I won't let you down,' he promised.

But Labda had seen Mrs Bacchiad's face when the man handed the baby back to her. She knew the woman wanted the baby dead. So that night she hid the child in a wooden chest. It slept safely and woke the next day still smiling.

Labda called the baby Cypselus – after the word meaning chest. Cypselus grew up a popular and groovy leader, while the Bacchiad family were hated in Corinth. The young man became king of Corinth – a strong king but a good-natured one. However, when it came to the Bacchiads he was quite, quite ruthless.

Cypselus was the rock that would roll down on those who ruled . . . and, like a rock, he crushed them. Just as the Oracle predicted.

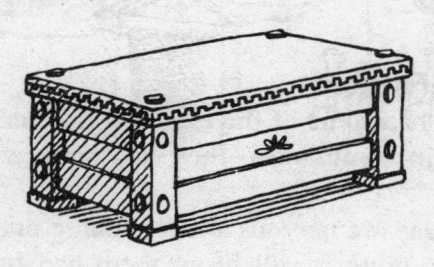

Did you know . . . ?
The Pythian Oracle at Delphi inhaled smoke from the burning leaves of certain trees to help them see into the future. The leaves gave off a drug that put them into a trance.

But at the Corinth Oracle there were cheats at work. There you could actually speak directly to a god! You spoke to the altar . . . and a voice boomed back from beneath your feet with the answer.

Was it a miracle? The visitors believed it was. But today's archaeologists know better. They found a secret tunnel that led under the altar. A priest could crawl along and lie under the feet of the visitor. He could listen to the questions and speak an answer through a funnel into a tube.

Greek superstitions

The Greeks had some of the cleverest thinkers of ancient times. Yet, in some ways, they had some very strange beliefs.

People today are nervous about walking under a ladder because they think it will bring them bad luck, or they touch wood to bring them good luck. The Greeks had their own strange superstitions. They believed. . .

1 Birds were messengers between earth and heaven, and the moon was a resting place for spirits on their way to heaven.

2 The Greeks believed that Hecate was the goddess of witchcraft and crossroads. She would appear at crossroads on clear nights, along with ghosts and howling phantom dogs. The Greeks left food at crossroads for her. (She was also asked for help with curing madness – the Greeks believed madness was caused by the spirits of the dead.)

3 The Greeks looked at the guts of dead birds and believed they could read the future from them.

4 They also thought there were spirits called 'daimons' around. Some were good and protected you; some were evil and could lead you into wickedness. Even clever people like Socrates believed in daimons. His own daimon warned him of trouble ahead . . . and it never let him down.

5 Sometimes the Greeks kept dead bodies in jars called *pithos*. But sometimes, they said, the spirits of the dead escaped from the jars and began to bother the living with illness and disease. These wicked spirits were called *keres*. The best way to stop the keres from getting into your house was to paint tar round your door frames. That way the keres would stick to the tar and not be able to get into the house.

6 The Greeks believed that if you dreamed about seeing your reflection in a mirror then you would die soon after. But don't worry, because you would soon be born again. According to some Greeks you are in three parts . . .

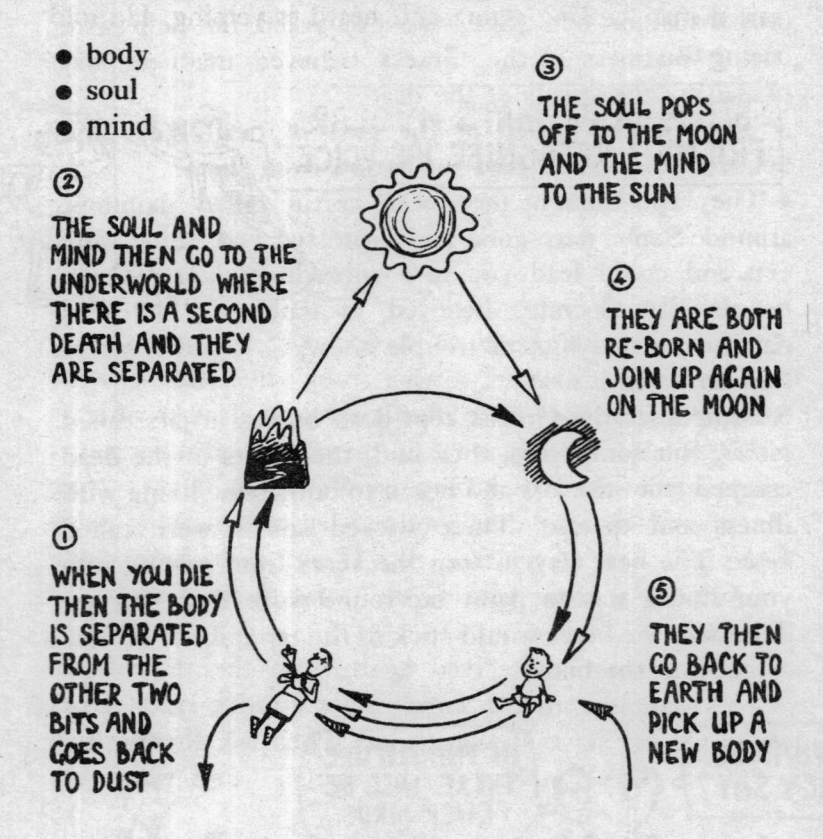

- body
- soul
- mind

② THE SOUL AND MIND THEN GO TO THE UNDERWORLD WHERE THERE IS A SECOND DEATH AND THEY ARE SEPARATED

③ THE SOUL POPS OFF TO THE MOON AND THE MIND TO THE SUN

④ THEY ARE BOTH RE-BORN AND JOIN UP AGAIN ON THE MOON

① WHEN YOU DIE THEN THE BODY IS SEPARATED FROM THE OTHER TWO BITS AND GOES BACK TO DUST

⑤ THEY THEN GO BACK TO EARTH AND PICK UP A NEW BODY

7 They also believed that the left side is bad – the right side is good. Many people still believe that today – they try to force left-handed children to write with their right hand, for example.

Potty Pythagoras
The famous teacher, Pythagoras, set up his own religion. The Pythagoreans believed that the soul lived on after death and went into another body. One day Pythagoras saw a man beating a dog and heard it yelping. He told the man . . .

'STOP! STOP! THAT'S MY DEAR FRIEND. I RECOGNISE HIS VOICE!'

In fact it wasn't safe to have anything to do with butchers or huntsmen — when they killed that cow or that deer they may have murdered your dead mother.

They also thought that if they behaved themselves they might come back as a great person. If they were naughty in this life they'd come back as something nasty — a pig, a dog, even a tree. And if you were really, really wicked you'd come back as the worst thing of all . . . a woman!

The Pythagoreans lived apart from the rest of the Greek people and had some rather strange rules. Does your teacher have strange rules? Then ask them which of these rules Pythagoras truly had. . . and which are false.

True or False
1 Don't eat beans.
2 Don't walk along the main street.
3 Don't touch the fire with an iron poker.

4 Don't touch a white cockerel.
5 Don't eat the heart of an animal.
6 Don't stand on your fingernail clippings.
7 Don't leave the mark of your body on a bed when you get up.
8 Don't look in a mirror beside a lamp.
9 Help a man to load something – but don't help anyone to unload.
10 Don't pick your nose with the fingers of your left hand.

Answer: 10 is false. All the rest are true. Some Greeks believed that beans contained the souls of the dead and would never eat them.

The ghostly Greeks

The groovy Greeks told the first ghost stories. But it was a Roman, Pliny, who first wrote this one down.

Dear Lucias

I have just heard this strange story which I think might intrest you.

In Athens there used to be a large and beautiful house which was supposed to be badly haunted. Locals told how horrid noises were heard at the dead of night: the clanking of chains which grew louder and louder. Until there suddenly appeared the hideous phantom of an old man who was a picture of filth and misery. His beard was long and matted, his white hair wild and uncombed. His thin legs were loaded with a weight of chains that he dragged wearily along with a painful moaning; his wrists were fastened by long cruel links, while all the time he raised his arms and shook his shackles in a kind of helpless fury.

Some brave people were once bold enough to watch all night in the house. They were almost scared out of their senses at the sight of the spook. Even worse, disease and even death followed those who had braved a night in that house. The place was shunned. A 'For Sale' sign was put up but no one bought it and the house fell almost to ruin and decay.

But Athenodorus was poor. He rented it even though he knew the story of the ghost. On his first night there he sat working. He heard the rattling chain and saw the gruesome old man. The ghost beckoned him with a finger. Athenodorus said he was too busy. The ghost grew angry and rattled his chains still more. The young man stood up and followed the spook.

When they reached the garden the spirit pointed to a spot in the garden - then vanished. Athenodorus marked the spot, went to bed and had a peaceful night's sleep.

Next day he went to the law officers and told them what he had seen. They dug at the spot the young man had marked and found a skeleton... bound in chains.

When the body had been given a proper burial, peace returned to the house at night.

Pliny

Think like a Greek
In the summer of 413 BC the army of Athens was in trouble. They were trying to beat the town of Syracuse with a siege. But one of their leaders had been killed and the other leader, Nicias, was poorly with a fever.

The Athenians decided to pack up and go home. Everyone agreed this was a good idea and they began packing to go. But that night there was an eclipse of the full moon. The soldiers said this was a sign from the gods.

A sign of disaster, some said. A sign that they should stay . . . or a sign that they should go? They couldn't agree. They asked their leader, Nicias.

'We will forget any plan to return home. We must wait for the next full moon,' Nicias said.

He waited 27 more days. What happened?
1 Nicias died and the army went home.
2 They suffered disaster anyway.
3 The Syracuse army surrendered.

Answer: 2 The extra 27 days gave the Syracuse navy time to block off the river with rows of ships chained together. The Athenian ships couldn't get out of the river to get their army back home. Their army had to march across the land instead. The enemy were waiting and the Athenian army was wiped out. The ones who weren't killed were made into slaves. This disaster was the end of Athens as a great state . . . and all because of an eclipse of the moon and the superstitious nature of a Greek general.

Live like a Greek

Polybius' Checkerboard
The Greeks were also very groovy with numbers. Polybius, born in 200 BC, was a Greek historian of Rome. He was one of 1,000 hostages taken to Rome in 168 BC. His main history books contained 40 volumes, but he also had time to invent this code, now known as Polybius' Checkerboard.

Each letter has a pair of numbers – the horizontal (across) number followed by the vertical (up-down). So, 'B' is 1-2, but F is 2-1. The word 'Yes' is 54 15 43. Get it?

	1	2	3	4	5
1	A	B	C	D	E
2	F	G	H	I/J	K
3	L	M	N	O	P
4	Q	R	S	T	U
5	V	W	X	Y	Z

Then work out this . . .
44 23 15 22 42 15 15 25 44 15 11 13 23 15 42 11 33
11 53 24 32 11 33 14 15 42 12 42 34 45 22 23 44 44
23 15 21 24 42 43 44 43 45 33 - 14 24 11 31 44 34
22 42 15 15 13 15.

Answer: The Greek teacher Anaximander brought the first sun-dial to Greece.

Did you know . . . ?
Polybius' Checkerboard may have been a good way of sending secret messages. But a Greek called Histiaeus found a better one!

He was imprisoned by the Persians but was allowed to send a letter to his cousin Aristagoras. The Persians studied the message carefully. They could see no code or secret meaning. The message was a perfectly harmless letter. They let a slave take the letter to Aristagoras.

As soon as the slave arrived he said to Aristagoras, 'Shave my head.' Aristagoras shaved the slave's head. Tattooed on his scalp was the real message. 'Lead a rebellion against the Persians.' Cool, eh?

Make a pinhole camera

The Greeks also invented other groovy devices which are still important to us today. One of the cleverest was the camera obscura – or the 'pinhole' camera. A Greek artist covered a window with a dark material, then punched a small hole through. An upside-down image of the scene was seen on the inside wall and traced by the artist.

You could have a go at making your own, slightly smaller version:
1 Make a box of black card, 20 x 10 x 10 cm.
2 Make a small pinhole in black paper at one end.
3 Place grease-proof paper across the other end.
4 Hold it up to a bright scene.
5 The scene will be 'projected' on to the grease-proof paper.

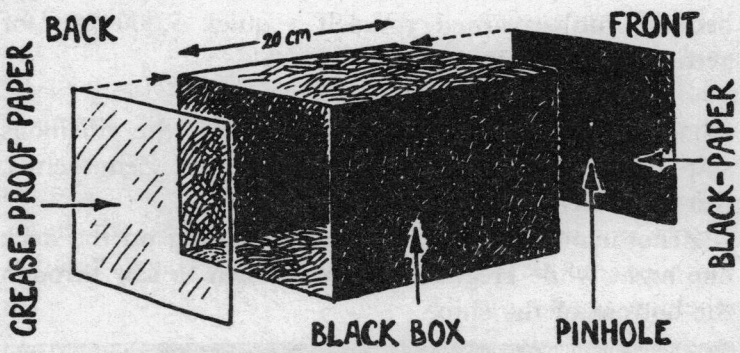

Note: this image will be upside-down – you may have to stand on your head to get the best view!

Making a dodgy drachma

The Greeks had banks. There are no records of bank robbers . . . but there were people who tried to cheat the banks out of lots of money. Here's how to do it. . .

1 Go to the bank and say, 'I want 10,000 drachmas to buy a ship. I'll fill it with corn and sell it on the other side of the Mediterranean. When the ship returns with the money for the corn I'll pay back the loan.'
2 The bank agrees. The Greek banks even agree that if the ship sinks (and you lose all their money) then you don't have to pay them a thing.
3 You buy a cheap ship and put a little bit of cheap corn in it. You spend about 5,000 drachmas and keep the other 5,000 drachmas for yourself.
4 Just as the ship reaches deep water you saw through the keel at the bottom of the boat. This will make it sink.
5 When the boat begins to sink you jump in the lifeboat, paddle back home and say to the bank, 'Sorry, you've lost your 10,000 drachmas!' and have a good laugh because you've earned yourself a quick 5,000 just for getting your feet wet.

Good idea, eh? And it nearly worked for the villainous ship owner, Hegestratos, and his partner, Zenothemis. But it all went wrong at stage 4.

Zenothemis kept the passengers chatting on the deck one night while Hegestratos crept down to saw through the bottom of the ship.

One of the passengers heard the noise and went down to investigate. Hegestratos was caught and had to escape. He fled along the deck and jumped into the waiting lifeboat. Or rather he *tried* to jump into the lifeboat. It was dark. He missed the little boat, fell in the sea . . . and drowned. Served him right.

The ship reached the shore safely and the bank got Zenothemis to pay back the money. So Hegestratos ended up dead . . . not rich.

Let the punishment fit the crime

Alexandria was a city in Egypt but ruled by the Greeks. Around 250 BC they had a set of laws which might give some idea of how the Greek law worked.

Can you match the crime to the punishment? Just remember the law wasn't completely fair. Especially if you were a slave.

Crime	Punishment
1 A free man strikes another free man or free woman.	a) A hundred lashes
2 A slave strikes a free man or free woman.	b) Fine of 100 drachmas
3 A drunk person injures somebody else.	c) A hundred lashes
4 A free man threatens another with wood, iron or bronze.	d) Fine of 100 drachmas
5 A slave threatens another with wood, iron or bronze.	e) Fine of 200 drachmas

Answers: 1d) 2c) 3e) 4b) 5a)

If a master didn't want his slave to receive the 100 lashes then he had to pay 200 drachma, or 2 drachma a blow.

If you argued with a fine then you could go to court. But be careful. If you lost then you had to pay double for crime 1 or treble for crime 4.

Woe for women

Being a slave in ancient Greece wasn't much fun. Being a woman wasn't too groovy either. The Spartan women lived like men – the Athenian women lived like slaves. They were told what to do and what not to do – and they didn't have anything like the freedom that the free men enjoyed . . .

GREEK GOOD WIFE GUIDE

A WOMAN SHOULD	A WOMAN DOES NOT
• STAY AT HOME • BE BROUGHT UP WITH SLAVES AND LEARN HOUSEHOLD SKILLS • LEARN TO SPIN, WEAVE, COOK AND MANAGE SLAVES • HAVE A HUSBAND - CHOSEN BY HER FATHER - WHEN SHE IS 15 • WORSHIP THE GODDESS HESTIA	• VOTE • BUY OR SELL ANYTHING WORTH MORE THAN A SMALL MEASURE OF BARLEY • OWN ANYTHING OTHER THAN HER CLOTHES, JEWELLERY AND SLAVES • LEAVE THE HOUSE EXCEPT TO VISIT OTHER WOMEN OR GO TO RELIGIOUS FESTIVALS AND FUNERALS

Groovy girls

The women of Attica, the region surrounding Athens, were different from the women living in Athens. They helped their husbands in the fields. They also had a curious way of preparing their daughters for marriage.

Girls aged about 13 were sent to the Brauron temple of the goddess, Artemis. There they prepared to be mature young women, and good wives, by doing what?

1 Learning how to fire bows and arrows, to throw spears, to mend armour and sharpen swords.
2 Praying to the goddess for wisdom, and learning the secret spells to keep husbands happy and healthy.
3 Running and dancing through the woods with no clothes on pretending to be she-bears.

> *Answer:* 3 The idea was they got their wildness 'out of their systems' before they settled down to marriage. The Brauron temple proved very popular with Greek girls around 370 - 380 BC.
> However, girls, you should *not* try this at your local place of worship — you'd only get arrested, or photographed by the boys in your class, or catch pneumonia ... or all three.

Dress like a Greek
Instead of running naked through the local woods, you could find out what it was like to be a groovy Greek by dressing like one. Here's a simple groovy costume to make.

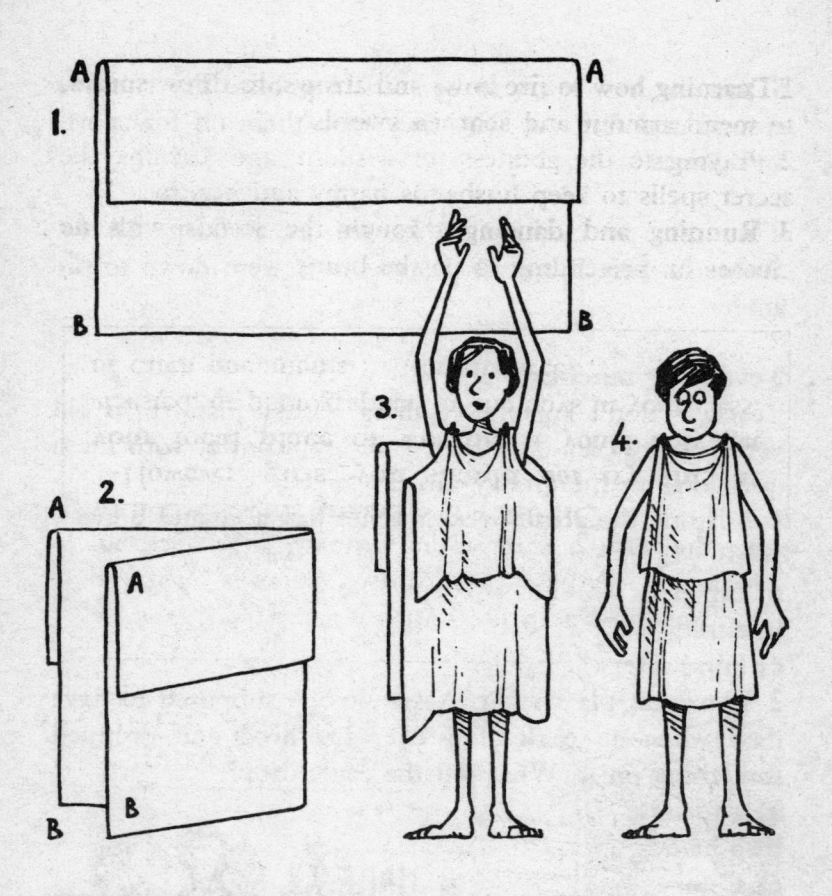

(**Warning:** Only suitable for summer weather.)
1 Fold an oblong cloth as shown – do *not* use Mum's best sheets for this – use Dad's.
2 Fold it again.
3 Wrap it round the body and pin it at each shoulder – the Greeks didn't have safety pins, but you can cheat and use a couple.
4 Fasten the open side with pins. Tie a belt around the waist. See picture 4 . . . here's one I made earlier.

5 You are now ready to be seen in public. Try running around and find out why they took them off for sports and games.

This sort of clothing is known as a *Doric Chiton*. Women's were the same design but it went down to the ankle.

Test your teacher
Teachers don't know everything – they just try to kid you that they do. Test their true brain power with these questions on the groovy Greeks...

1 Aristotle the great Greek teacher had a favourite meat. What was it?
a) camel
b) turkey
c) horse liver

2 The great playwright, Aeschylus, is supposed to have died when an eagle flew over his head and dropped something on it. What did the eagle drop?
a) a tortoise
b) a hare
c) a stone

3 As well as the Olympic games there were games in Isthmia. The winners at the Isthmian games were given a crown as a prize. What was the crown made of?
a) celery
b) rhubarb
c) gold

4 Before clever Aristotle came along, the Greeks had a strange belief about elephants. What was it?
a) an elephant has no knee joints so it goes to sleep leaning against a tree
b) elephants never forget
c) eating elephant meat makes you strong

5 Which team sport did the Ancient Greeks enjoy that we still play today?
a) hockey
b) soccer
c) volleyball

6 The Greek teacher, gorgeous Gorgias, said that 'nothing exists' ... not even himself. He nearly didn't. He had a peculiar birth. Where was he born?
a) in his dead mother's coffin
b) on a mountain in a snow storm
c) on board a sinking ship

7 The Spartan youths tried out their military training by doing what for their town?
a) becoming secret police and murdering troublemakers
b) mending roads and keeping the streets clean
c) becoming servants in old people's homes and cooking for them

8 How far did the Greek explorer, Pytheas, sail?
a) Britain and the North Sea
b) Crete in the Mediterranean
c) America and the Atlantic

9 The Greeks invented a new weapon in the 4th century BC. They set fire to inflammable liquids then threw them over enemy ships or enemy cities. What is this weapon called?
a) Greek fire
b) Zeus's revenge
c) flaming dangerous

10 A sacred plant was sprinkled on graves. But we don't consider it sacred today. What is it?
a) parsley
b) cabbage
c) garlic

Answers: The answer to every question is a).
- If your teacher scored 0 to 5 they need to go back to school.
- 6 to 9 is pretty good.
- If they scored 10 they probably cheated and read the book before you did.

Test yourself

Now test yourself. See how many answers you can remember by arranging the following into the right order . . .

A	B	C
The playwright, Aeschylus,	invented a new weapon called	hockey
A sacred plant	sailed to	a camel
Aristotle, the great Greek teacher,	died when hit on the head by	an elephant going to sleep leaning against a tree
A Greek sportsman	was born in	a tortoise
A Greek sailor	was sprinkled on graves and called	the secret police
A Spartan youth	enjoyed the team sport called	celery
The Greek explorer, Pytheas,	won a crown made from	Greek fire
The Greek teacher, Gorgias,	believed in	the North Sea
A winner at the Isthmian games	trained in	parsley
An early Greek person	enjoyed meat from	his dead mother's coffin

89

Die like a Greek

What's up, Doc?
The earliest Greek doctor was said to be called Aesculapius. But, since he was supposed to be the son of a god, he probably didn't exist.

But his followers, the Asculapians, did exist. They didn't work from a hospital, they worked from a temple. Most of their patients recovered with rest, sleep and good food. But Asculapians liked people to think they were gods so the patients had to say prayers and make sacrifices.

The temple was famous because no one ever died in the temple of Aesculapius and his doctor-priests! How did they manage this?

They *cheated*. If someone was dying when they arrived then they weren't allowed in. And if they started dying once they got inside they were dumped in the nearby woods.

I'M FEELING A LOT BETTER!

The doctor-priests were in it for the money. They warned patients that if they didn't pay, the gods would make them sick again. And they advertised. Carvings in the ruins show the doctor-priests made fantastic claims . . .

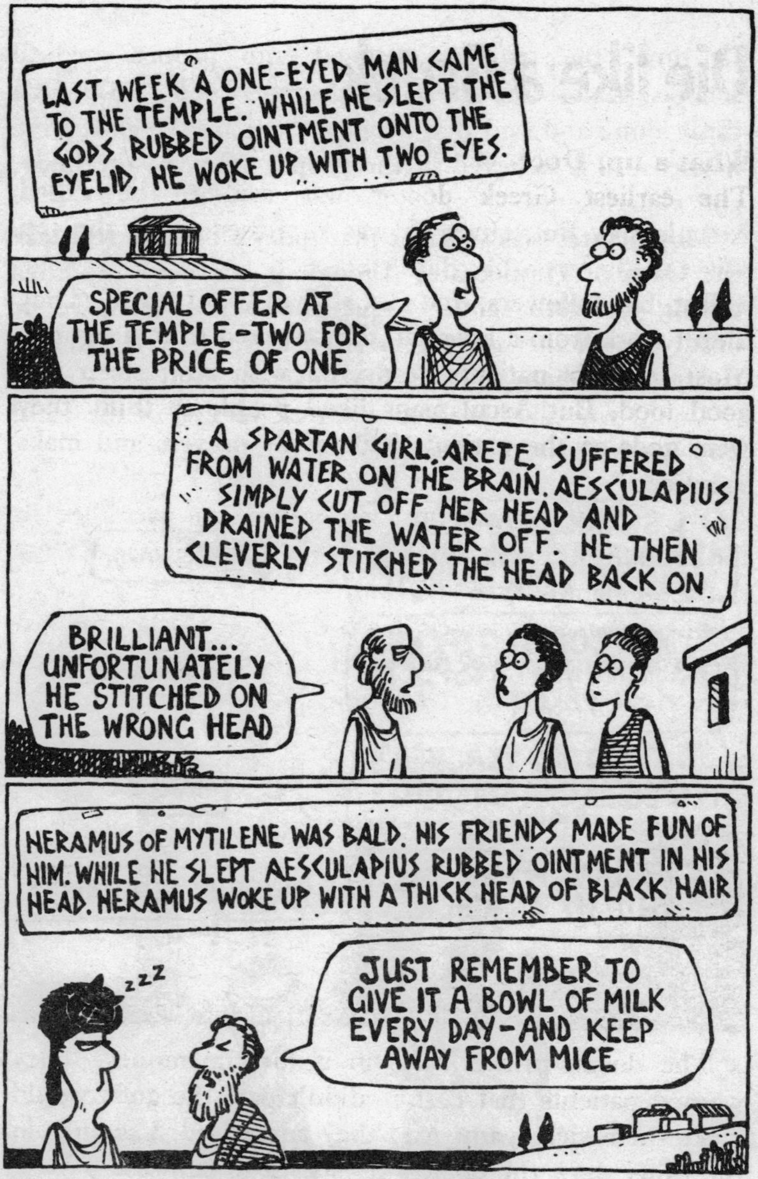
LAST WEEK A ONE-EYED MAN CAME TO THE TEMPLE. WHILE HE SLEPT THE GODS RUBBED OINTMENT ONTO THE EYELID, HE WOKE UP WITH TWO EYES.
SPECIAL OFFER AT THE TEMPLE-TWO FOR THE PRICE OF ONE
A SPARTAN GIRL, ARETE, SUFFERED FROM WATER ON THE BRAIN. AESCULAPIUS SIMPLY CUT OFF HER HEAD AND DRAINED THE WATER OFF. HE THEN CLEVERLY STITCHED THE HEAD BACK ON
BRILLIANT... UNFORTUNATELY HE STITCHED ON THE WRONG HEAD
HERAMUS OF MYTILENE WAS BALD. HIS FRIENDS MADE FUN OF HIM. WHILE HE SLEPT AESCULAPIUS RUBBED OINTMENT IN HIS HEAD. HERAMUS WOKE UP WITH A THICK HEAD OF BLACK HAIR
ZZZ
JUST REMEMBER TO GIVE IT A BOWL OF MILK EVERY DAY-AND KEEP AWAY FROM MICE

In time, the temples changed into proper medical schools. Later, the great Hippocrates (460 – 377 BC) came along and said that magical cures by the gods were nonsense. He believed in the proper study of the body, and experiments.

Hippocrates was so great that today's doctors still take the Oath of Hippocrates (though it has been modified during the 20th century) and promise, 'I will give no deadly medicine to anyone if asked . . . I will use treatment to help the sick but never to injure.'

Could you take the groovy Greek version of the oath? You would have to swear . . .

I SWEAR BY APOLLO, AESCULAPIUS AND ALL THE GODS, TO KEEP SECRETS	THAT'S HARD
TO RESPECT MY TEACHER AS MUCH AS I RESPECT MY PARENTS	EASY
TO TREAT MY TEACHER'S FAMILY LIKE MY OWN FAMILY	HARD
TO SHARE MY INCOME WITH MY TEACHER	YOU MUST BE JOKING!

But Hippocrates wasn't perfect. He said there were 91 bones in the body – now we know there are 206!

He also believed in 'bleeding' as a cure. A young man with a rumbling tummy was 'bled' by Hippocrates until he hardly had any blood left in his body . . . and he recovered!

One test for a lung disease was to shake the patient – and listen for the splashing inside.

Old Doc Hippo was a bit of a whinger. He complained that, 'If a patient gets worse or dies, people always blame the doctor.'

Still, *you* would complain if you had to do what Hippo had to do. Hippo took samples of . . .
- vomit
- snot
- ear wax
- pee
- tears
- infected wounds

. . . and he tested them. But he didn't test them in a laboratory with chemicals the way modern doctors can. He tested them by what?
1 colour
2 boiling them with rhubarb juice
3 tasting them

Answer: 3 Either the doctor or the patient had to taste the sample.

Hippo and his followers also practised cutting into the skull to drain fluids off the brain. But he wasn't the first to do this . . . there is evidence that Stone Age people did this operation. (Would you like to be operated on by a surgeon with a flint axe?)

The superstitious Greeks kept the piece of bone as a good-luck charm. It was supposed to keep you safe from disease.

But Hippo said some things which doctors today, every day, still say to their patients. . .

> *Fat people die sooner than thin people.*

Hippo also said how doctors should look and behave . .

> *A doctor must be careful not to get too fat. Someone who can't look after his own fitness shouldn't be allowed to look after other people's.*
>
> *Secondly he should be clean, wear good clothes and use a sweet (but not too strong) scent. This is pleasant when visiting the sick.*
>
> *He must not look too grim or too cheerful – a grim man will worry the patient while a laughing man may be seen as an idiot.*

And he must have been a good doctor because he lived to the age of 99 years.

Medical monster
Not every doctor was as good and unselfish as Hippocrates. Menecrates of Syracuse was much more grasping and cruel. He was especially fond of really sick patients because he could blackmail them.

> CAN YOU CURE ME DOC?
> COULD IF I WANTED
> THEN CURE ME!

> SIGN THIS PAPER AND YOU WILL BECOME MY SLAVE IF I CURE YOU

> AND IF I DON'T SIGN?
> THEN YOU DIE OF COURSE

> I'LL SIGN

Medical manure
Of course, if you didn't want to go to a doctor like Menecrates then you could always try curing yourself. The great thinker, Heraclitus, did this.

He fell ill with dropsy – a disease where you swell up because there's too much fluid in your body. He decided to test his doctors by asking them a riddle. 'How do you make a drought out of rainy weather?' The doctors didn't know the answer – neither do I. Do you?

So Heraclitus decided to cure himself. He reckoned

the best way to get rid of too much liquid was to apply heat. In his farmyard he had a pile of rotting animal droppings – manure. The centre of the manure pile was warm.

Heraclitus buried himself up to the neck in the manure . . . and died.

Warning: Do *not* try this at home. If the manure doesn't kill you, your mother probably will – and your friends won't speak to you till you've had a hundred and five baths.

Perilous plague

One thing Greek doctors could do nothing about was the plague. The plague which killed hundreds in Athens in 430 BC . . .

- probably came from Egypt
- came so suddenly that rumours said the enemies had put poison into the water tanks
- started with a headache and sore eyes
- made breathing difficult and turned the throat red
- made victims begin to sneeze
- caused sickness when the infection moved to the stomach
- caused the temperature to rise so a plague victim couldn't stand wearing any clothes
- made victims grow terribly thirsty so they threw themselves into wells
- covered them in spots
- usually killed the victim
- often caused survivors to lose their memory:

> CONGRATULATIONS, YOU'RE BETTER!

> BETTER THAN WHAT?

Birds of prey wouldn't normally go near the dead bodies as they lay waiting to be buried. The birds that did always died.

The historian, Thucydides, said...

> *People died whether they had treatment or not. What cured one person often killed another. Some caught it by nursing others and they died like sheep. In fact this was the greatest cause of death. Corpses lay where they died on top of each other and the dying lurched around the streets and wells in their crying need for water.*

> I FEEL SICK

> MAYBE IT WAS SOMEONE YOU ATE

Some families burned their dead. Thucydides also said that passing funerals often dumped their body on somebody else's funeral fire... then ran off!

Deadly Docs: 1

King Pyrrhus of Greece had a deadly doctor in 278 BC. The doc wrote to the Romans and said . . .

> DEAR FABRICUS,
> I AM THE DOCTOR TO PYRRHUS, IF YOU ARE WILLING TO PAY ME I WILL POISON THE KING

But Fabricus sent the letter straight back to Pyrrhus, his enemy, and explained. . .

> UNTO KING PYRRHUS, GREETING,
> YOU HAVE MADE A BAD CHOICE OF FRIENDS AND ENEMIES, YOU ARE AT WAR WITH HONEST MEN, BUT HAVE WICKED AND UNFAITHFUL MEN ON YOUR SIDE. AS YOU WILL SEE FROM THE LETTER THERE IS SOMEONE IN YOUR CAMP WHO PLANS TO POISON YOU. WE ARE TELLING YOU THIS BECAUSE WE DO *NOT* WISH TO BE BLAMED FOR SUCH A TREACHEROUS ACTION. WE WISH TO END THIS WAR HONOURABLY ON THE BATTLEFIELD.
> FABRICUS

King Pyrrhus found the traitor and gave the doctor a taste of his own medicine, as it were, by having him executed. He was so grateful to the Roman enemies that he set his Roman prisoners free without a ransom.

Deadly Docs: 2

If you can't poison the enemy king then at least you can *stop* him taking medicine that would get him *better*. How? *Tell* him he's being poisoned by his doctor . . . even if he *isn't!*

> THAT ASPIRIN WILL MAKE YOUR HEADACHE WORSE

That's what Darius did to his enemy, Alexander the Great. Alexander was sick and received a letter from the double-crossing Parmenio. Like Fabricus's letter, it said . . .

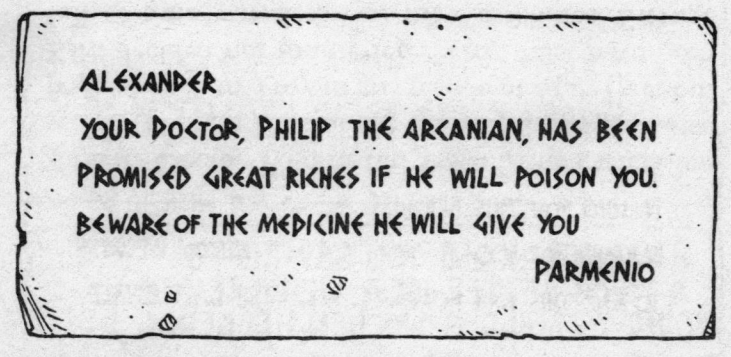

> ALEXANDER
> YOUR DOCTOR, PHILIP THE ARCANIAN, HAS BEEN PROMISED GREAT RICHES IF HE WILL POISON YOU. BEWARE OF THE MEDICINE HE WILL GIVE YOU
>   PARMENIO

That evening, Doctor Philip arrived with a cup full of medicine. Alexander had the letter by his bedside. Was it really poison in the cup?

Alexander did a brave thing. He handed the letter to Doctor Philip. At the same time he drank the cup of medicine in one swallow.

Philip was impressed. 'But how do you know it wasn't poison?' he asked.

'I don't know about poison,' Alexander told him, 'but I do know about men. And I know you would never betray me, my friend.'

Alexander recovered. Not all doctors were cunning and treacherous.

Medical mystery

Which 'doctor' travelled through time to help the Greeks at Troy? (Clue: He gave them the idea about building a wooden horse.)

Answer: Doctor Who in the 1980s British television series. (Captain Kirk of the Starship Enterprise also popped back to Troy in an episode of *Star Trek*, but Kirk decided not to interfere. Troy must have been full of time travellers and their machines. Strange that Homer didn't mention them in his poems!)

A WOODEN HORSE YOU SAY. THAT'S A MUCH BETTER IDEA. WE WERE GOING TO BUILD A WOODEN HEDGEHOG

Odd Olympics

The groovy Greeks liked nothing better than a contest. The first Olympic contests were simple foot races. The first few Olympics had just one race on one day – a race of about 190 metres or the length of the stadium.

A second race – twice the length – was added in the 14th Olympics, and a still longer race was added to the 15th competition, four years later. But new events were added until the meeting lasted five days. There was even a Junior Olympics for kids.

- The bad news, girls . . . females were banned from the ancient Olympics.
- The bad news, boys . . . clothes were banned for the male athletes.

Choose your champion

You may wish to try an Olympic contest against the class next door. First you need to have a contest in your own class and choose your champion to represent you. Then go and cheer your champion as they compete against rival class champions.

Here's what to do. First choose your judges. They must train as judges (or referees) for ten months before the Olympics. They must also be honest. (You could have a problem finding an honest adult.) Agree the starting time and place and let the competitors battle it out.

- foot race – 200 metres
- double foot race – 400 metres
- standing long jump – with a kilo weight held in each hand to swing you through the air

- quoit-throwing (nearest to a fixed spot wins)
- javelin

After the contest . . .
1 Give the winners crowns made from the branches of a wild olive tree that grows in a sacred grove. (If you can't find one then make cardboard crowns from a sacred cornflakes packet.)
2 Call out the victor's name and country to the assembled crowds. (Or just phone the local newspaper.)
3 When the victor returns to their home they enter through a special gap knocked in the city wall. (Might be better if you *didn't* knock down the school wall. That's there for a purpose – to stop wild pupils escaping.)
4 The victor is treated with special favours – they either pay no taxes, or have free meals at the president's house for life. (Perhaps you could offer your victor a lifetime of free school dinners.)

5 Don't forget to cheer the loser. Losers have feelings too. (An Olympic wrestler called Timanthes lost his strength as he grew older. He was so upset he lit a big fire – then threw himself into it.)

Some groovy Olympic games you might not like to try

Mule-racing – smelly.

Relay – a bit hot. The god, Prometheus, stole fire from the gods and brought it down to earth for humans. But the humans had to escape from the other avenging gods. They ran with torches. The Olympic relay was run with flaming torches instead of batons, in memory of Prometheus. If the torch goes out your team loses. And if you grab the wrong end of the torch from the last runner . . . ouch!

IT'S NOT MY HAND I'M WORRIED ABOUT!

Four-horse chariot race – dangerous. The poet Homer described an accident. . .

> *Eumelos was thrown out of the chariot beside the wheel. The skin was ripped from the elbows, nose and mouth, and his forehead smashed in over the eyebrows. His eyes filled with tears and his powerful voice was silenced.*

A bit rougher than your school rounders match, eh?

Hoplite racing – heavy, but not groovy. Wearing full armour and carrying weapons, this was hard work – try running with a couple of dustbins strapped to your back and that's how it might feel.

HOPLITE, NOT LIGHT HOP!

Trumpeters' competition – deafening.

Pancration ... what? Pancration was a bit of a mixture of boxing and wrestling. The only rule was that there were no rules, apart from no biting and no gouging out the eyes. Just flatten the opponent. You could ...
- strangle
- kick
- arm-twist
- jump up and down on your opponent.

Quite good if you're a winner. Painful for a loser.

Boxing – ordinary old boxing? Yes, harmless little fisticuffs – unless you do it the ancient Greek way, as the horrible historical story of Creugas and Damoxenos shows ...

The Greek Guardian
still only 20 obols
Creugas the Corpse Claims Crown

In the Olympic heavyweight championship yesterday Damoxenos, the Dark Destroyer, beat challenger Creugas . . . and lost the title!

In a sensational contest the two men were both defending their unbeaten records. A crowd of two thousand sat on the grass in the afternoon sunshine to enjoy a fight to the end. They didn't know what an end it was going to be.

Boos

Big Damoxenos was booed as he stepped on to the grass and had leather wrapped around his mighty fists. The handsome Creugas was cheered as he stepped forward. The voice of the referee rang out across the grassy circle.

'Remember, slaps with the open hand, punches with the fist or blows with the back of the hand are allowed. Kicking is permitted, but no head butting. Understand?'

'Yes sir,' Creugas answered boldly. Big Damoxenos just grunted.

'The fight goes on without a break until one man has had enough,' the little ref went on. 'Show you are beaten by raising your right hand in the air. Understand?'

Damoxenos just sneered. 'I'll not need to remember that,' he boasted. 'I'll not be surrendering.'

Hammer

The crowd booed again as the referee stepped back. 'Box!' he cried and Damoxenos lunged forward. He swung his fist like a mighty hammer at Creugas's head but the young man jumped back and flicked a fist at the champion's head.

That was the pattern of the fight. Big Damoxenos lumbering round, swinging huge punches but unable to catch the slippery Creugas. Just as the crowd was growing restless, the sun sank down and the referee called a halt.

'We cannot have a draw,' he cried. 'The contest will be decided by a single blow struck by each man.'

First

The crowd seemed to like that and they closed in to get a better view.

'You go first, wimp,' Damoxenos growled. The big man held his arms by his sides – the crowd held its breath.

Creugas struck a hammer blow to the champion's head. The big man just laughed. 'My turn.'

The young man shook his head and waited for the blow that would surely knock him senseless. It didn't.

Instead the big ox hit Creugas cruelly under the ribs with straight fingers. His sharp finger nails tore through the young man's skin. He pulled back his hand and jabbed again. This time he tore out the challenger's guts.

The crowd gasped as Creugas fell lifeless to the ground.

Cheat

The ref ran forward. 'One blow is all that is allowed. You took *two* blows, Damoxenos, you cheat. I hereby disqualify you. I declare that Creugas is the champion!'

The crowd cheered with joy. The new champ was not available for comment.

His manager said, 'The boy done well. Deserved that win. We'll have a few drinks later to celebrate.'

Creugas will always be remembered as a champion who had guts.

Did you know . . .? Olympically speaking

1 There was a fine for cheating. The cheat had to pay for an expensive statue of the god Zeus. And at Olympus there were an awful lot of Zeus statues before the Greek Olympics ended. There must have been a lot of cheats.

2 The main form of cheating was to have a really good set of horses in the chariot race then have a bet that you would *lose* the race. You made sure you lost the race by pretending to whip the horses to go faster . . . while secretly tugging at the reins to slow them up. This 'pulling' of horses to win money still goes on today.

3 The Greek Olympics were banned by the rotten Romans. The Romans didn't much like sport when they conquered the Greeks. The Romans preferred their own groovy 'games' . . . like fights to the death between gladiators . . . and they built huge coliseums to stage the contests. But they let the beaten Greeks keep their Olympics until miserable Roman Emperor, Theodosius, abolished them in 394 AD.

4 The Greek Olympics had competitions in music, public speaking and theatre as well.

5 The Olympics vanished for 1500 years. They were revived in 1896 by Pierre de Coubertin, a young French nobleman, and since then they have been staged every fourth year. The ancient Greek Olympics were held in honour of Zeus, and all wars would cease during the contests. The Olympics came first. Sadly, in the modern Olympics, war came first; the games stopped during World War I and World War II (1916, 1940, 1944).

6 A cook, Coroibus of Elis, was the first recorded winner.

7 The boy athlete, Pisidorus, took his mum to the Olympics. Because women were banned, she had to be disguised as his trainer.

8 ... and, talking about trainers. There are quite a few 'Nikes' at modern Olympics. But did you know that Nike was the goddess of victory, who watched over all athletic contests?

9 A sports arena was one 'stadion' (600 Olympian feet, 190 metres) long. That's why we have sports 'stadiums' today. The competitors raced up and down, not round and round.

10 The poet Homer described a race between Odysseus and Achilles. Odysseus was losing and said a quick prayer to the goddess, Athena. She not only made Achilles slip – she made him fall head first into cattle droppings. He stood up spitting cow dung – and lost the race, of course.

Funny food

Sacrificial snacks
A sacrifice is *supposed* to be a groovy gift to the gods. 'Here you are, gods, here's a present for you. I'm being nice to you, so you will be nice to me, won't you?'

When the Greeks sacrificed an animal to a god, they roasted it and they ate it. That's a bit like buying your mum a box of chocolates then scoffing them yourself.

- The greatest honour was to have some roasted heart, lungs, liver or kidney from the sacrificed animal.
- The best meat was shared around.
- Everything left was minced together and put into sausages or puddings – but the important people didn't bother with those.
- This didn't leave very much for the gods to eat, you understand. Just the tail, the thigh bones and the gall bladder.

The Greeks even mixed the blood and the fat together and stuffed it into the bladder of the animal. They then roasted and ate this little treat. Would you like to try this to see what the Greeks ate? (Without all the mess of sacrificing a cow, of course. That can make a terrible mess on the living-room carpet.) Then go to your local butcher's shop and ask for it. But what do you ask for?

1 haggis
2 black pudding
3 sausage

DON'T YOU THINK YOU'RE TAKING THE SACRIFICE THING A LITTLE TOO FAR?

> *Answer:* 2 Black pudding. The Greeks roasted it while we tend to fry it in slices, but really it's the same thing.

Did you know . . .?
Vegetarians in ancient Greece wouldn't sacrifice animals to the gods. Instead they sacrificed *vegetables* – groovy, eh?

Munching Milon
Milon was a wrestler. He also thought he was pretty groovy. Before one Olympic contest he walked around the stadium with a live young bull on his shoulders.

He fancied a snack after all that effort, so he killed the bull and ate it. He finished the whole bull before the day was out.

But maybe there are some gods on Olympus with a sense of fair play. Because, in the end, Milon got what he deserved. *Exactly* what he deserved.

It started with him showing off again. He split open a tree with his bare hands . . . but his hand became stuck in the split. Try as he might he couldn't get free. When a pack of wolves came along they licked their chops and moved in on Milon.

What did they do to Milon? Just what Milon did to the young bull – except they probably didn't cook him first.

Foul food
The Greeks ate the meat of sacrifices but didn't eat a lot of meat in their normal day-to-day lives. One historian

said, 'The Greeks had meals of two courses; the first a kind of porridge – and the second a kind of porridge.'

In fact it wasn't quite that bad. The 'porridge' was more a sort of paste made up of lentils, beans and corn all ground up with oil – vegetable oil, not the sort of oil garages put in cars.

The peasants had some olives, figs, nuts or goats-milk cheese to add a bit of taste. They washed it down with water or goat's milk.

After about 500 BC the rich started to eat more meat than the peasants – goat, mutton, pork or deer – and drink wine rather than water. But what else did they eat of the following?

WHAT A PIG!

1. SEA URCHINS
2. THRUSHES
3. YORKSHIRE PUDDING
4. PIGS WHICH HAVE DIED OF OVER EATING
5. PEACOCK EGGS
6. LUPIN-FLOWER SEEDS
7. SPAGHETTI
8. GRASSHOPPERS
9. TURNIPS
10. HONEY CAKES

> *Answer:* All except 3 and 7

Spartan soup

You might not have enjoyed living in Athens and eating grasshoppers and thrushes. But you could have been worse off. You could have lived in Sparta.

The Spartans had a disgusting concoction called Black Broth. They mixed pork juices with salt and *vinegar* into a sort of soup.

The Athenians made some very cruel comments about Spartan food. Athenaeus said, 'The Spartans claim to be the bravest people in the world. To eat food like that they'd *have* to be.'

Another Athenian said, 'It isn't surprising the Spartans are ready to die on the battlefield – death has to be better than living on food like theirs.'

The groovy Greek guzzler

Archestratus wrote the first ever cookery book in Europe. It was written in *verse* and probably meant to be recited at feasts – not used as a recipe book. It contained some quirky bits of advice to eaters and to cooks. Archestratus seemed a rather grumpy man with strong views on some foods . . .

> *A Pontic fish, the Saperde,*
> *Is poor and tasteless and it smells.*
> *To those who eat this thing I say,*
> *Both you and it can go to hell!*

And Archestratus had his own favourite foods. He liked to rubbish more popular dishes . . .

> *Now some men like the taste of beef,*
> *They sing the praises of the cow.*
> *While I would rather get my teeth*
> *Into the belly of a sow.*

But Archestratus saved his nastiest comments for foreign cooks who ruined good Greek food with their recipes . .

> *If your food you want to waste,*
> *Take a Bass fish from the sea,*
> *Find a cook with awful taste*
> *Like the cooks from Italy.*
>
> *Syracuse has bad cooks too*
> *Spoiling Bass in sauce of cheese.*
> *Or in pickles, taste like glue,*
> *Keep away from cooks like these.*

Just as well he didn't live to taste our modern versions of Italian delights. He might have written a horrible verse like . . .

> *Spaghetti hoops that come in tins*
> *Belong in deep and dusty bins.*
> *As for tasteless plastic pizza*
> *Simply leave it in your frizza.*

Groovy Greek growing-up

Bother for babies
From 500 – 200 BC there was a ritual way of treating babies. Would *you* survive?

Father inspects baby. Is it fit?
Yes Go to 1.
No Go to 2.
Don't know Go to 5.

1 If you have too many boys then they'll have to split up your land when you die. Too many girls will cost you money. Do you want to keep it?
Yes Go to 6.
No Go to 2.

2 Put the baby in a pot (a pithos), then leave baby on a hillside to die. Do you care?
Yes Go to 4.
No Go to 3.

3 Baby dies before it's a week old.

4 Let a childless couple know what's going on. They will get to it before the cold or the wolves do. Baby lives with foster parents.
Go to 6.

5 Father will 'test' the baby by rubbing it with icy water, wine or urine (yeuch). Does it survive?
Yes Go to 6.
No Go to 3.

6 The baby is one of the family. Tell the world with an olive branch on the door if it's a boy, a piece of wool for a girl.
Go to 7.

7 Hold the *Amphidromia* ceremony. When baby is seven days old, sweep the house and sprinkle it with water. Father holds baby and runs round hearth with it while family sings hymns.
Go to 8.

8 When baby is ten days old have the naming ceremony. (A boy is named after his grandfather.) Congratulations – you've made it . . . unless disease or plague or war or something else gets you!

The good news: Boys didn't go to school until they were seven – girls didn't have to go to school at all.

The bad news: You didn't add up with numbers. You added up with letters – a = 1, b = 2, c = 3 and so on.

> MUM'S GIVEN ME A 2-9-7 6-9-7 FOR DINNER! WONDER WHAT 4-1-4 8-1-4?

But do *you* know what number BAD + HEAD make?

Answer: 214 + 8514 = 8728

> WHAT DOES *BAD* AND *HEAD* MAKE?

> A CASE FOR THE DOCTOR SIR!

The really bad news:
Boys took a slave to school with them. No, *not* to do their work. The job of the slave was to make sure the boy behaved himself. If he didn't then the slave would give him a good beating.

Test your teacher
The Greeks loved thinking about things – the science of thinking about things became known as 'philosophy'. But it was a thinker from Italy who came up with the most curious thoughts – Zeno of Elea. The Greeks loved talking and thinking about Zeno's 'problems'. Test your teacher with this sneaky (and Greeky) question . . .

Surviving school dinners

Have you ever been to school dinners and seen nothing you fancy? What happens? You go hungry.

The Lydians went hungry for a very long time because there was a famine. They decided to do something about the problem. They discovered that the more you think about food the hungrier you get. So they invented games to take their minds off food. They played dice and knucklebones.

The games were so interesting they didn't notice they were hungry. The next day they ate whatever they could find but didn't play games. This went on for 18 years! Games one day, food the next.

So, if you don't fancy a school dinner then play knucklebones. You need five ankle-joints from *cloven-footed* animals. (They make neat cubes of bone.) There are several cloven-footed animals – bison, pigs, goats, antelopes and sheep. If any of those appear on a school-dinner menu then you might just be in luck.

If your school cook slaughters her own wildebeest in the kitchens, then ask her for the little cube-shaped bones from the ankle joint. If she *doesn't* then you'll just have to use small cubes of wood like dice.

Knucklebones: 'Horse in the Stable'
Players: One or more players.
You need: Five knucklebones (or wooden cubes).
Rules: Put four knucklebones on the ground. Each one is a 'horse'.

Put the left hand near them with the fingers and thumb tips spread out and touching the ground. The gaps between the fingers are the 'stables'.

One knucklebone is tossed into the air with the right hand.

Before catching it the player must knock one 'horse' into a 'stable' with the right hand – that is, they must flick a knucklebone into a gap between the fingers.

With the right hand, catch the knucklebone that was thrown in the air.

Repeat until all four 'horses' are in their 'stables' – no more than one 'horse' to a 'stable'!

If all four are put in their 'stables' then move the left hand away from the 'horses'. Toss the throwing stone into the air with the right hand, pick up all four horses with the right hand, and catch the throwing stone in the right hand.

If the turn ends with a full 'stable', or if the player makes a mistake, pass the turn to the next person.

The first to 'stable' all the 'horses' ten times is the winner!

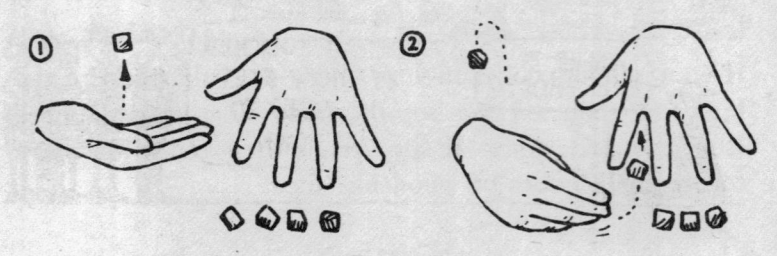

The school Olympics
Greek children invented games like knucklebones that are still played in some parts of the world today. In fact you may even have played some of the games yourself. If you haven't, and want to play like a groovy Greek, then here are the rules for six games.

Ostrakinda
This is a game for two teams that is still played in Italy, Germany and France. You need: A silver coin. Paint one side black with poster paint – this side is 'Night'. The plain side is 'Day'.

Rules: 1 Divide into two teams – the 'Nights' and the 'Days'.
2 Spin the coin in the air.
3 If it lands black side up then the Nights chase the Days – and if it lands silver side up the Days chase the Nights.

Cooking pot
Rules: 1 Choose someone to be 'It'.
2 'It' is blindfolded and sits on the ground.
3 The others try to touch or poke 'It'.
4 'It' aims to touch one of the teasers with a foot.
5 Anyone touched by a foot becomes 'It', is blindfolded and sat on the ground.

Bronze Fly
A sort of Greek Blind-man's Buff. A Greek described it

> They fastened a head-band round a boy's eyes. He was then turned round and round and called out, 'I will chase the bronze fly!'
> The others called back, 'You might chase him but you won't catch him.'
> They then torment him with paper whips until he catches one of them.

ISN'T THAT A BULL WHIP?

Ephedrismos
Rules: 1 A player is blindfolded and gives a second one a piggy-back.
    2 The rider then has to guide the player to a target set on the ground.
    3 If the player succeeds then he becomes the rider. This could become a competition where pairs race to reach the target.

ARE YOU SURE THIS IS THE WAY TO THE TARGET?

Greecket

The Greeks also played ball games where you throw a ball at a 'wicket', rather like cricket without a batsman.

We just have pictures of these games that have been painted on Greek vases, but we don't have their written rules. Make up your own rules – maybe they played like this . . .

1 Stand on a mark a fixed distance from the wicket.
2 Take the ball and have ten attempts to hit the wicket.
3 The opponent stands behind the wicket (like a wicket-keeper) and throws the ball back to you every time.
4 Then you stand behind the wicket while your opponent has ten tries.
5 The one who has the most hits on the wicket from ten throws is the winner.
6 Try again from a different mark.

It looks (from the vase paintings) as if the loser has to give the winner a piggy-back ride.

WHY IS IT ALWAYS THE BIG KIDS WHO ARE GOOD AT GAMES

Kottabos

Rules: 1 Take a wooden pole and stand it upright.
2 Balance a small metal disk on top of the pole.
3 Leave a little wine in the bottom of your two-handled drinking cup.
4 Grip the cup by one handle, flick the wine out and try to knock the disk off the top of the pole.

(Would you believe grown-up Greeks played this silly game at parties?)

You can try this with a cup and water and a 50p coin on the end of a broom handle . . . but *not* in your dining-room, please.

Puzzle your parents

So your parents think they're smart, do they? Give them this simple test to check their brain-power. All they have to do is answer 'Groovy Greeks', 'Terrible Tudors' or 'Vile Victorians' . . .

Who had these toys or games first? The Greeks, the Tudors or the Victorians?

1 puppets moved by strings
2 draughts
3 tug of war
4 dolls with moving parts

5 model chariots
6 yo-yos
7 babies' rattles
8 spinning-tops
9 see-saws
10 bowling hoops

Answer: *All* were first played by the *Greek* children. Any other answer is wrong. How did your parents score?

10 probably cheating
6–9 quite good – for an adult
3–5 go back to school – or read 'Groovy Greeks'
0–2 never *ever* let this parent offer to help with your homework. Your pet hamster could do better. In fact a *dead* hamster could do better.

The Romans are coming

Bodge-up at Beneventum!
As the Greek armies grew weaker, the Romans grew stronger. At first the groovy Greeks won all the battles – but lost a lot of men each time. The Romans learned from their mistakes and got better every battle, until finally, in 275 BC...

PYRRHUS WAS DESPERATE TO STOP TWO LARGE ROMAN ARMIES JOINING UP

I HAVE A PLAN

A PLAN?

WE ATTACK THE ROMANS FROM BEHIND AT FIRST LIGHT

THAT'S A BIT SNEAKY PYRRHUS

SNEAKY IS MY MIDDLE NAME

HOW DO WE ATTACK FROM BEHIND, THEY'RE IN FRONT OF US?

WE GO THROUGH THE FOREST TONIGHT

IT'LL BE DARK

TAKE TORCHES AND THE VERY BEST ELEPHANTS. IT CAN'T FAIL

IT CAN

IT DID. FOR A START IT WAS FURTHER THAN THEY THOUGHT

ME TORCH HAS GONE OUT

MINE TOO. I'M LOST

THE SUN CAME UP. IT LET THEM SEE THEIR WAY. IT ALSO LET THE ROMANS SEE THEM

OOPS!

> AND WORSE WAS TO COME. A YOUNG ELEPHANT WAS MADDENED BY THE ROMAN SPEARS. IT CHARGED AROUND THE BATTLEFIELD LOOKING FOR IT'S MUM. IT ALSO TRAMPLED ITS GREEK OWNERS
>
> MUMMY!
>
> RESULT: ROMAN 1 - GREEKS AND ELEPHANTS UNITED 0

Jumbo facts

1 The first Greek to come across an elephant army was Alexander the Great when he invaded India.

2 Apart from trampling and terrifying the enemy, elephants gave a good shooting platform for archers.

3 The Greeks used elephants supplied by India. The elephant trainers came with them. The elephants grew from babies with their trainer. No one else could command an elephant because it only understood the trainer's Indian language.

4 An elephant trainer was important to the Greeks and he was paid more than the average soldier.

5 A year after the bodge-up at Beneventum the Greeks arrived at Argos. In the battle an elephant lost its driver. The creature ran round the battlefield until it found him, dead on the ground. It picked him up with its trunk and rested the body across the tusks before carrying its dead master off the battlefield. And it wasn't too bothered who it trampled to death as it crossed the battlefield – Greek friends as well as Roman enemies.

Pathetic Pyrrhus

King Pyrrhus met a particularly pathetic end in his battle to defeat the Romans. In 274 BC he was fighting at the siege of Argos when a peasant with a pike hurt him. The peasant didn't hurt the King very much, you understand, but Pyrrhus was furious and turned to smash the pike man with his sword.

Poor Pyrrhus reckoned without the women of Argos. They had climbed up to the roof tops to watch the battle. They must have been like proud parents watching a school football match. You know, the sort who stand on the touchline and shout things like, 'Get stuck in, our Timothy!' And, 'Come on ref – get your eyes tested!'

Anyway, who should be watching Pyrrhus attacking the pike man peasant? The peasant's mum.

'Hey! That's my little boy you're trying to kill, you big bully!' she cried. The woman tore a tile off the roof and flung it at Pyrrhus.

Well, the woman was either an Olympic-standard discus thrower . . . or very, very lucky. The tile gave Pyrrhus a crack on the back of the neck, just below the helmet. His neck was broken and he dropped dead from his horse.

If there'd been newspapers in those days, *The Argos Chronicle* would have enjoyed that story. Imagine the headlines . . .

PROUD PIKE PEASANT'S PARENT POTS PATHETIC PYRRHUS

. . . perhaps?

Epilogue

After the groovy Greeks came the rotten Romans. The Romans were supposed to be an even greater people than the Greeks. After all, they eventually ruled over half the world – including Britain.

But the Romans were pretty rotten compared to the Greeks. Their games weren't great sports events like the Olympics – they were just an excuse to watch humans kill animals, animals kill humans, animals kill animals and humans kill humans. In boxing, for example, the Greeks bound their hands with leather bands like boxing gloves. The Romans bound their hands with leather bands – but put vicious spikes in them.

The Greek plays had been exciting and interesting. The Romans tried to copy them but were looking for more action and violence. Roman plays eventually killed people on stage for real.

One story about the take-over of Greece by the Romans gives a good example of what the world lost when the rotten Romans took over from the groovy Greeks . . .

Archimedes was a brilliantly clever Greek. When the Romans attacked his people in the city of Syracuse (211 BC) Archimedes used his great and groovy brain to invent wonderful new weapons.

For two years the Romans were kept out of the city as the inventor created 'death-rays' – giant mirrors that reflected the sun on to Roman ships in the harbour and set them on fire – and huge catapults that drove them off.

But at last the Romans broke through the Greek defences and brought terror to the citizens of Syracuse as they killed and stole from the houses. The Roman commander had given one strict order, however: 'Find Archimedes – but don't hurt the great man.'

At last a Roman soldier burst into Archimedes' house. The inventor was in the middle of an experiment and was too busy to bother with a small matter like an invasion at that moment.

The Roman was puzzled. Why was this old man ignoring him?

The Roman became angry. How *dare* this old man ignore him?

The Roman lost his cool. He killed the defenceless inventor. With one blow he destroyed one of the cleverest men the world has known.

The Roman soldier was punished for disobeying the commander's order not to harm Archimedes. But that didn't bring the old man back. Just as none of even the greatest Roman achievements could bring back the glory of the Greeks.

The rotten Romans ruled – the groovy Greeks went to their graves. That's horrible history for you.

GROOVY GREEKS

GRISLY QUIZ

Now find out if you're a
groovy Greek expert!

Gruesome Greek Quiz

Simply answer 'Yea' for yes or 'Nay' for no to these facts about the grisly Greeks.

1 In the story of Troy, King Agamemnon sacrifices his daughter to the gods. Would that have really happened in ancient Greece?
2 A slave called Aesop told great stories such as 'The Tortoise and the Hare'. He was richly rewarded by the Greek priests.
3 The people who lived in the city of Sparta were super-tough kids. One Spartan boy hid a stolen fox cub under his tunic and didn't let on, even though the fox ate the boy's guts away.
4 In Draco's Athens (c. 600 BC) the laws were strict and you could be whipped for stealing a cabbage.
5 Athens' ruler Peisistratus (605–527 BC) arranged to have himself attacked so the people would feel sorry for him.
6 Teacher Socrates taught his students not to believe in the old Greek gods. Socrates was hanged.
7 General Alcibiades (450–404 BC) wanted people to notice him. Once he cut off his dog's tail to get a bit of attention.
8 The Greeks read the future using the guts of dead birds.
9 Hecate was the Greek goddess of crossroads. Greeks left food at crossroads for her.
10 The Greeks painted the doors of their houses red with blood.

WHAT DO THEY SAY?

IN THE FUTURE THERE WILL BE FEWER BIRDS

Suffering Spartans

The Spartans were the toughest of all the Greek peoples – and it was extra-tough for Spartan kids.

Here's a Spartan rule book with some of the words missing. Get the answers right – or take a savage Spartan punishment!

The missing words, in the wrong order, are: no clothes, hair, herd, thistles, mountains, whipped, baths, girls, bite, beaten.

1. A bad serving-child will receive a ____ on the back of the hand.
2. A sickly baby will be taken to the ____.
3. A new bride must cut off her ____ and dress like a man.
4. Children caught stealing food will be ____.
5. A child belongs to the state of Sparta. At the age of seven children will join a ____.
6. A Spartan child may have only a few ____ a year.
7. In processions, dances and temple services girls must wear ____.
8. If a Spartan child is cold in winter, then they may sleep under ____.
9. Good Spartans are ____ at the altar of the goddess Artemis.
10. ____ are to be trained for fitness BY running, wrestling, AND throwing quoits and javelins.

Test Your Teacher Quiz

Everyone studies the Greeks at school. Greek history lessons were even around when your teachers went to school, so they should know the answers to these ten quick questions.

1 General Alcibiades hated the Greek gods and damaged

their statues. He smashed off what part of the statues? (Clue: he only did this to the male gods)

2 The superstitious Greeks did not like dreaming of seeing your own face in a mirror. What did they think you would do soon after? (Clue: never see your face in a mirror again!)

3 Around 375 BC the girls of Attica went to the local temple and ran round the woods pretending to be bears. What did they wear? (Clue: don't try this at the North Pole)

4 Greek teacher Aristotle had a favourite food that you will probably never eat. What? (Clue: unless you are stranded in the Sahara desert)

5 Playwright Aeschylus died (it is said) when an eagle dropped an animal on his head. What? (Clue: a slow death?)

6 Greek teacher Gorgias was born in a strange place. In his mother's what? (Clue: he was dead lucky to be alive, but Mum wasn't.)

7 Greeks invented a nasty weapon. It was a liquid that caught fire as soon as it landed and set fire to everything it touched in open air. What was it called? (Clue: not Roman water but...)

8 Aesculapius was a Greek doctor. Some of his cures worked. Some of the stories of other cures are plain daft. How did he cure (they say) water on a girl's brain? (Clue: she got it in the neck)

9 Doctor Hippocrates practised cutting out a circle of the skull to drain fluids off the brain. But why did the patient take home the circle of bone? (Clue: like a rabbit's foot?)

10 Some vegetarian Greeks refused to sacrifice animals to the gods. What did they sacrifice instead? (Clue: obvious really!)

Answers

Gruesome Greek Quiz

1) Yea. At the time of the Trojan Wars, not only were children sacrificed but bits of them were eaten too. Aren't you glad you weren't around?

2) Nay. In fact they took him to the top of a cliff and threw him off. It seems a few of his stories upset them.

3) Yea. This was a popular story told by the Spartans. Of course it may have just been Spartan boasting and a big fib. But it's a warning – don't go sticking foxes (or bears or budgies) up your jumper!

4) Nay. Draco was much tougher than that! The punishment for pinching an apple or a cabbage was death! By the way, the punishment for idleness was also death! (Think of all those dead teachers in your school if we still had that law!)

5) Yea. Peisistratus staggered into Athens bruised and bleeding and said the city would suffer if its people didn't protect him. But he had arranged the attack on himself. The people of Athens were tricked into protecting him ... even though they hated him.

6) Nay. He was sentenced to death by poisoning. And he had to drink the poison himself. Which he did. So he carried out his own death sentence. Why not ask your teacher to demonstrate how a brave teacher behaves?

7) Yea. Alcibiades was a pretty good Athenian general but switched sides to the Spartan enemies. But the Spartans didn't trust the traitor much. In the end he was murdered, shot full of Spartan arrows, and his dog would have wagged its tail in joy – if Alcibiades hadn't cut it off, that is.

8) Yea. Don't try this at home with your pet parrot. You'll make a right mess on the carpet. Stick to reading horoscopes in the newspaper.

9) Yea. She always had a pack of howling dogs with her. (If you want to carry on this ancient Greek habit then why not leave a tin of dog food at your nearest crossroads, eh? Seems a shame for Hecate to get all the grub.)

10) Nay. They painted them black with tar! They believed evil spirits would stick to the tar and be kept out. Messy.

Suffering Spartans

1) Bite. Younger boys had to serve older boys. If the younger boy did something wrong he could be given a nasty nip!

2) Mountains. Babies were left up a mountain to die if they failed a health check.

3) Hair. And a bridegroom had to pretend to carry his

bride off by force.

4) Beaten. Children were kept hungry and encouraged to steal food! (Spartans thought sneakiness was a handy skill in battle.) If the kids were caught stealing, they'd be beaten for being careless enough to get caught!

5) Herd. The toughest child was allowed to become leader and order the others about.

6) Baths. Stinky Spartans!

7) No clothes. So they didn't get fancy ideas about fine clothes.

8) Thistles. Children slept on beds of rushes that they gathered themselves from the river bank. In winter they could mix a few thistles in with the reeds – the prickles were supposed to give them a feeling of warmth!

9) Whipped. A horribly historical way to prove you were a good Spartan! The one who suffered the most lashes was the toughest. Some bled to death.

10) Girls. So don't mess with a Spartan miss.

Test Your Teacher Quiz

1) Their naughty bits. Alcibiades knocked off the naughty bits on the statues of the naked gods. Ouch!

2) Die. Mind you, some people are so hideous they'd probably die if they saw themselves in a mirror awake! (Bet you know people like that!)

3) Nothing. This was supposed to prepare them for being grown women. The crazy chases were supposed to

get the last wild bits of fun out of them before they became boring adults.

4) Camel. Maybe we should start serving camel at posh tea parties. You turn to your guest and say, 'One hump or two?'

5) A tortoise. We do not know how the tortoise was after the accident. If it lived it was probably a bit shell-shocked though.

6) Coffin. Georgias's mother died and was popped in a coffin but somehow the baby was born anyway. He grew up and taught his students, 'Nothing exists – not even me!' If I'd been his student I'd have just skived off school then!

7) Greek Fire. Even today no one is sure how Greek Fire was made. But it was nasty stuff. Not the sort of thing you'd want to spray on your barbecue.

8) He cut off her head. After the water drained off he sewed the head back on. Hummmm! Believe that and you are ready for a new head yourself!

9) For luck. The superstitious Greeks kept the bone as a good-luck charm. It was supposed to keep you safe from disease.

10) Vegetables. They killed carrots, cracked corn and carved cabbages cruelly and then they probably battered some poor beans brutally. Vile vegetarians, how could they?

INTERESTING INDEX

Where will you find 'cow dung', 'ear wax', 'snot-tasting' and 'manure' in an index? In a Horrible Histories book, of course!

Achilles (warrior) 108, 116
Aegisthus (boyfriend of Clytemnestra) 28, 31, 33-4
Aeschylus (playwright) 22-3, 86, 89
Aesop (storyteller) 36-7
Agamemnon (king) 24, 27-33
Alcibiades (general) 58-9
Alcmaeon (body-slicer) 8
Alexander the Great (Macedonian king) 9, 61-3, 99-100, 125
Apollo (god) 64, 92
archaeologists 35, 69
Archestratus (author of first-ever cook book) 112-13
Archimedes (inventor) 9, 127-8
Argos (Greek city) 125-6
  women of 126
Aristotle (philosopher) 9, 61, 86-7, 89
Artemis (goddess) 44, 83
Asclepius (god) 51
Asculapians (doctor-priests) 90-1
assassinations 45, 48, 59
Athena (goddess) 34, 45, 108
Athenians 8-9, 46-53, 55-9, 61, 76, 82-3, 112

Bacchiad family (rulers) 66-9
Beneventum, battle of 124-5
blackmailers 95
blood, drinking 40
Boetians (group of ancient Greeks) 59-60
Brauron temple 83-4

Cassandra (Trojan princess) 32-3
Charidemus (general) 18-23
cheats 66, 69, 79, 88, 90, 107
checkerboard (code invented by Polybius) 77-8
clothes 38, 58, 84-6
Clytemnestra (wife of Agamemnon) 24, 26-34
comedies 8, 23
Corinthians 56-7, 66-7, 69
cow dung 108
Crete 7, 10
Creugas (boxer) 104-6
Crito (pupil of Socrates) 51
Croesus (king) 7, 65-6
Cronos (old chief god) 11-14
Cypselus (king) 69

137

daimons (spirits) 71
Damon (Trojan traitor) 19-21
Damoxenos (boxer) 104-6
Darius (Persian king) 53, 99
Dark Ages 10, 34, 38
dead bodies
　cutting up 8
　in jars 71
death-rays (giant mirrors) 127
democracy 9, 52
Dioneces (general) 43
doctors 90-100
dogs
　cut-off tails 58
　phantom 71
Dorians 10
Draco (early Greek ruler) 46-7

ear wax, tasting 93
earthquakes 35-6
eclipses 7, 76
Egypt 55, 62, 81, 96
Electra (daughter of Agamemnon) 25, 31-4
elephants 87, 124-5
epics 22-6
Eumelos (chariot-racer) 103
Euripedes (playwright) 22

Fabricus (Roman leader) 98
fines 81-2, 107
flame-throwers 60
food 19-20
　foul 110-13
　stealing 40
Furies (avengers) 34

games 117-23

ghosts 45, 57, 62, 64, 71, 74-5
gods 10-15, 22, 33, 36
　avenging 34, 103
　baby-eating 11-14
　believing in 50
　sacrifices 29-30, 109-10
　ship of 56-7
　speaking 55, 64, 67, 69
　throwing up 13
　whipped at altar of 44
　wooden 37
Gordian knot 63
Gorgias (teacher) 87, 89
guts
　eaten by foxes 42
　reading 71
　tearing out 106

Hades (god) 15
Hecate (goddess) 71
Hegestratos (cheat) 80-1
Helen (wife of Menelaus) 22, 24-5, 28-9, 32, 35
Hellespont (stretch of water) 53-4
hemlock (poison) 50-1
Hera (goddess) 7
Heraclitus (philosopher) 95-6
Herodotus (historian) 40, 54, 56
Hestia (goddess) 83
Hippocrates (doctor) 92-4
Homer (poet) 7, 22-3, 34, 61, 100, 103, 108

The Iliad (epic poem) 22
Iphigenia (daughter of Agamemnon) 25, 30-1, 33, 35

Knucklebones (game) 117-19

Labda (mother of King Cypselus) 66, 68-9

laws 46–7, 52, 81
legends 10, 15
Leonidas (king) 43
Lydians 117

Macedon 9, 61–3
magicians 45
manure 96
Marathon, battle of 8, 53
marriage 39, 83–4
masks 25
medicine 90–100
Menecrates (blackmailer) 95
Menelaus (king) 22, 24–5, 28, 32
Milon (wrestler) 110
money 37, 79, 81, 90, 107
moon 70, 72, 76
Mycenaeans 7, 10

naughty bits 25, 58
Nicias (leader) 76
Nike (goddess; yes, really) 108

Odysseus (king) 108
Olympic Games 6–7, 9, 64–5, 87, 101–8, 110, 126–7
Olympus, Mount 14, 107
Oracle of Delphi 29, 37, 55, 64–6, 68–9
Orestes (son of Agamemnon) 27, 31–4

Paris (Trojan prince) 17, 24
Pausanius (general) 44–5
pee, tasting 93
Peisistratus (tyrant) 8, 47–8
Peloponnesian wars 8, 57–60
Pelusium, battle of 54–5
Pericles (leader) 8
Persians 8–9, 43–5, 53–62, 66, 78

Philip (father of Alexander) 61–2
philosophy 116
plague 8, 96–7, 114
Plato (philosopher) 50
plays 6–7, 22–6, 36, 127
Pliny (Roman writer) 74–5
Plutarch (writer) 47
poetry 7, 22, 24, 61, 63
poison 50–1, 96, 98–100
police, secret 87
Polybius (historian) 77–8
Poseidon (god) 14, 36
priests 64–6, 69, 90
Prometheus (fire-stealer) 15, 103
punishments 46–7, 73, 81–2
Pyrrhus (king) 98, 124, 126
Pythagoras (philosopher) 73
Pytheas (explorer) 88–9

rituals 114
Romans, rotten 9, 77, 98, 107, 124–8

sacrifices 48, 51, 64, 90
    children 35
    eating 109–10
    girls 26, 29, 35
Salamis, battle of 55–7
scalps 41, 78
Scythians 40–1
skulls 55, 94
slaves 37–8, 46, 52, 76, 81–3
snot-tasting 93
Socrates (philosopher) 50–1, 71
Spartans 7–8, 24, 38–46, 48, 50, 53, 55, 59, 82, 87, 89, 91, 112
starvation 45
stealing 40–1
stomach 8, 13, 96

139

sun 7, 43, 72, 78, 106, 124
superstitions 70-2
Syracuse 8, 58-9, 76, 95, 113, 127-8

tails
  cutting off 58
  eating 109
tattoos 78
teachers 5-6, 15, 50-1, 61, 73, 86-7, 92, 116
Thales (scientist) 7
Thebans 8
Themistocles (military leader) 55-6
Theodosius (Roman emperor) 107
Thermopylae, battle of 8, 42-4
thistles, sleeping on 39
Thucydides (historian) 97
thunderbolts 14
Timanthes (wrestler) 102
toilets 10
tortoise
  dropped on head 86
  racing 116
  stewed 65-6
tragedies 23
Trojan wars 7, 16-24, 34-6, 61

underworld 15
Uranus (god) 14
vomit, tasting 93

weapons 59-60, 127
wooden horse 7, 16-23, 32, 35, 100
World Wars 107
writing 7, 22

Xerxes (Persian king) 8, 43, 45, 53, 55, 57

Zenothemis (cheat) 80-1
Zeus (new chief god) 12, 14-15, 107

Terry Deary was born at a very early age, so long ago he can't remember. But his mother, who was there at the time, says he was born in Sunderland, north-east England, in 1946 – so it's not true that he writes all *Horrible Histories* from memory. At school he was a horrible child only interested in playing football and giving teachers a hard time. His history lessons were so boring and so badly taught, that he learned to loathe the subject. *Horrible Histories* is his revenge.

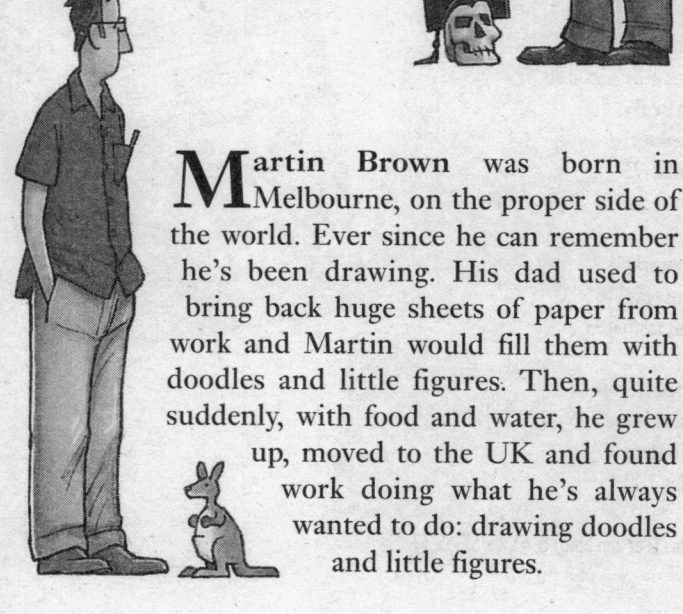

Martin Brown was born in Melbourne, on the proper side of the world. Ever since he can remember he's been drawing. His dad used to bring back huge sheets of paper from work and Martin would fill them with doodles and little figures. Then, quite suddenly, with food and water, he grew up, moved to the UK and found work doing what he's always wanted to do: drawing doodles and little figures.

Make sure you've got the whole horrible lot!

HORRIBLE HISTORIES
AWESOME EGYPTIANS
Terry Deary & Peter Hepplewhite
Illustrated by Martin Brown
ISBN: 978 0439 94403 8   £4.99

HORRIBLE HISTORIES
MEASLY MIDDLE AGES
Terry Deary Illustrated by Martin Brown
ISBN: 978 0439 94401 4   £4.99

HORRIBLE HISTORIES
ROTTEN ROMANS
Terry Deary Illustrated by Martin Brown
ISBN: 978 0439 94400 7   £4.99

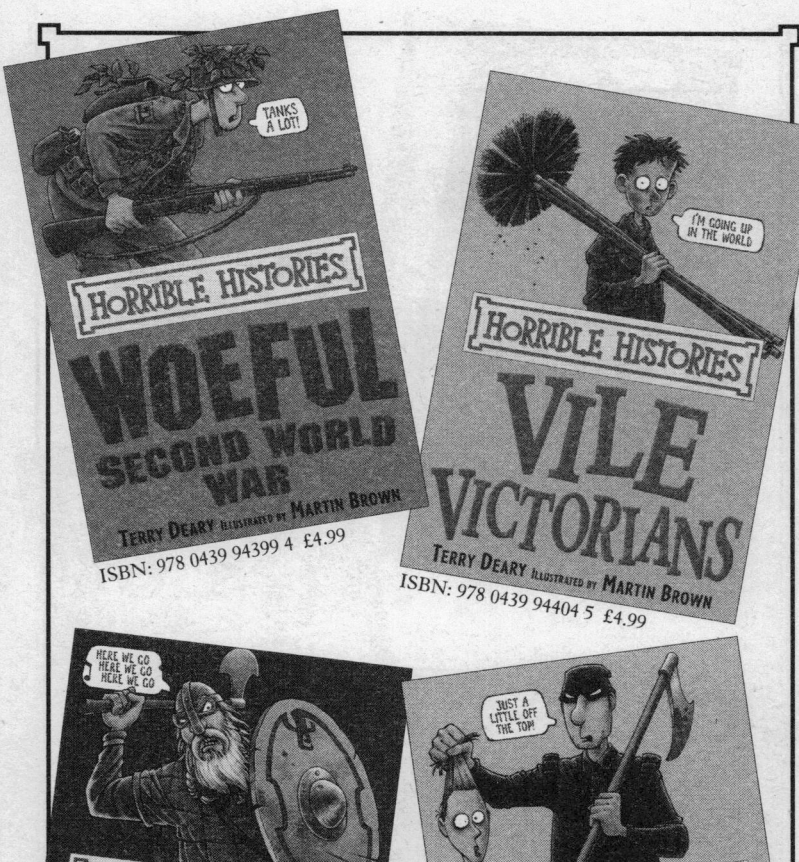

HORRIBLE HISTORIES

WOEFUL SECOND WORLD WAR
Terry Deary Illustrated by Martin Brown
ISBN: 978 0439 94399 4 £4.99

VILE VICTORIANS
Terry Deary Illustrated by Martin Brown
ISBN: 978 0439 94404 5 £4.99

VICIOUS VIKINGS
Terry Deary Illustrated by Martin Brown
ISBN: 978 0439 94406 9 £4.99

TERRIBLE TUDORS
Terry Deary & Neil Tonge
Illustrated by Martin Brown
ISBN: 978 0439 94405 2 £4.99

HORRIBLE HISTORIES HANDBOOKS
Pirates
IN BLOOD-CURDLING COLOUR!
Terry Deary Illustrated by Martin Brown
ISBN: 978 0439 95578 2 £5.99

HORRIBLE HISTORIES HANDBOOKS
Warriors
Terry Deary
ISBN: 978 0439 94330 7 £5.99

HORRIBLE HISTORIES HANDBOOKS
Knights
IN BLOOD-CURDLING COLOUR!
Terry Deary Illustrated by Martin Brown
ISBN: 978 0439 95577 5 £5.99

Don't miss these horribly handy handbooks for all the gore and more!